So Great a
Cloud of Witnesses

Witnesses to God's
Activity in the World

David G. Rogne

CSS Publishing Company, Inc.
Lima, Ohio

SO GREAT A CLOUD OF WITNESSES

FIRST EDITION
Copyright © 2016
by CSS Publishing Co., Inc.

Library of Congress Cataloging-in-Publication Data

Names: Rogne, David George, 1934- author.
Title: So great a cloud of witnesses / David G. Rogne.
Description: FIRST EDITION. | Lima : CSS Publishing Company, 2016.
Identifiers: LCCN 2016017588 | ISBN 0788028359
Subjects: LCSH: Bible--Biography. | Christian biography.
Classification: LCC BS571 .R655 2016 | DDC 220.9/2--dc23
LC record available at https://lccn.loc.gov/2016017588

For more information about CSS Publishing Company resources, visit our website at www.csspub.com, email us at csr@csspub.com, or call (800) 241-4056.

e-book:
ISBN-13: 978-0-7880-2864-9
ISBN-10: 0-7880-2864-2

ISBN-13: 978-0-7880-2835-9
ISBN-10: 0-7880-2835-9

PRINTED IN USA

*This is for
Seth,
Ian,
Micaela,
Olivia,
And
Turner*

Table of Contents

Introduction

In the eleventh chapter of the book of Hebrews, the author lists many of the Old Testament heroes of faith and their exploits. Then, in his summation, he says, "since we are surrounded by so great a cloud of witnesses... let us run with perseverance the race that is set before us...." The author uses the analogy of a relay race to indicate that all people of faith have received a baton of faith, which they carry for a while, and then, as they depart the scene, they pass it on to the next generation. Those who have left the field have taken their seats in the arena as observers and encouragers of those who have come after. Each one who has gone before has contributed to the understanding of those who have followed, so that people of faith today have the benefit of the insights of those who have preceded them.

One of the insights of people of biblical faith is that God is active in history as he seeks to bring creation into conformity with his purpose. There have been those in every age who have discovered something of God's purpose and have attempted to pass it on. Sometimes, God's activity has been reported in supernatural terms, but as often, the activity of God is revealed in the faithful actions of human beings. For that reason, the Old and New Testaments are filled with the experiences of individuals who have discovered God's presence in their circumstances. Some, like Gideon, have led armies, or like David, have ruled nations. Some, such as the man born blind, have been so obscure that we do not even know their names. Some have thunderously spoken the truth they discovered, as was the case with prophets. Sometimes, they discover the truth by reflecting on their experiences, as when Jacob discovered God's grace when his own resources had come to an end. Sometimes, an individual's experiences are used to illustrate a truth discovered by someone else, as was the case with Daniel and Ruth.

This testimony to God's presence and purpose has continued into the post-biblical period as well. There have been witnesses to God's activity and purpose in every land and from every tradition. The author is most acquainted with the Christian tradition, and it is to that tradition that the author turns for witnesses to God's activity in the post-biblical period.

Biblical and post-biblical people of faith have often discovered that witnessing to the truth as they understood it was a costly proposition. Many experienced hostility, violence, and threat of death. Some were killed. Many of them were people of average talents, who addressed problems in their time, and either found solutions, or they found the courage to go on without solutions. It is their perseverance that makes them heroes. Their testimonies are what we need to hear.

I have attempted to choose witnesses from varied backgrounds so it may be seen that people from all walks of life are called to live faithfully and to witness to the truth as they understand it. The entire known story of some of these individuals, such as Joseph, the husband of Mary, may be just a few verses of scripture. Some, such as the wiseman and the Emmaus disciple, are not even named. Nevertheless, their witness is important. I have attempted to give life to the testimony of these less-well-known witnesses by giving them names and employing a little imagination. In every case, I have attempted to have the subjects tell their stories as they might have experienced them.

It is my hope that readers will gain an appreciation for the people of faith who are presented here, and humbly recognize the cost borne by so many to deliver the faith to us. They are a great cloud of witnesses. They have played their part in relaying the faith to subsequent generations, and they are now filling the stands in the heavenly arena, eager to see how we continue the race.

The Supplanter:
Jacob

Genesis 32:22—33:3

I've been a scrapper all my life. In fact, conflict was a characteristic of my life — even before I was born. I was born a twin, though far from identical. We created such a struggle in my mother's womb that she actually despaired of life, and she went to a seer to ask what was going on. The seer told her: "Two nations are in your womb, and two peoples, born of you, shall be divided; the one shall be stronger than the other, the elder shall serve the younger." That was an unheard of thing in our day, for the firstborn was expected to rule over the clan.

As you may imagine from what I've told you, I was the second born, and consequently, it didn't take me too long to realize that if I was going to get anywhere in life, it was going to be as a result of my own determination. From what my mother has told me, I was probably, by nature, determined and aggressive, for at the moment of birth, though my brother was firstborn, I was a close second, holding on to my brother's heel, as though to pull him back so that I could be born first. Because of that characteristic, I was named Jacob, meaning "supplanter." At this point it is hard to tell whether my subsequent life was a result of living up to my name, or whether my name was simply an accurate description of what I would have been anyway. I think that our names, whether chosen by us, or by someone else, have a lot to say about us. Take me, for instance; I've been called by many names, and they say a lot about me.

As I have told you, the first name I was given was Jacob, meaning "supplanter." My brother's name was Esau, meaning "red," because he was covered with red hair — not just on his head, but on his arms and legs, as well. Esau enjoyed hunting, as did our father. They were outdoorsmen; strong, physical, and gregarious. For that reason, Esau was the favorite of my father. Besides, Esau was firstborn, and when the time was right my father would give him the right of leadership, the major part of the inheritance, and his personal blessing. I lived under the shadow of all that while I was growing up.

I was different from my brother. I tended to keep to myself. I preferred raising flocks and herds to hunting, and not being as robust as my brother, I tended to live by my wits rather than by brawn. I took after my mother's side of the family, and consequently, she always looked out for my interests. That my brother should be entitled to the birthright by the accident of birth galled me continuously. One day, my brother had been out on a long hunt, and he came back to camp, famished. I was cooking a big pot of stew, which smelled delicious. My brother came in and asked for some of the stew, and I saw an opportunity to get something I wanted, so I said, "First, sell me your birthright." It was not his to sell, but if I were ever in a position to get it away from him, having his own verbal agreement would strengthen my position. Esau thought so little of the birthright that he said, "I am about to die of hunger. What good will the birthright do me if I die? Take it, and give me some stew." Whether Esau meant it or not, the transaction was made, and you see what a fool my brother was.

There was a second name I bore, though only for a little while. I had my brother's birthright; now I needed my father's blessing in order to prosper. My father, Isaac, had grown quite elderly. He was feeble and nearly blind. He just sat in his tent thinking about the good old days of hunting, and his mouth watered for game. So he called Esau and told him to go out and hunt game and prepare a savory dish, and that when Esau returned with it, my father would bless him. Esau started out.

My mother, Rebekah, had overheard the conversation, and she came and got me. She told me to kill a couple of goats, which she would then cook in a savory sauce, such as my father loved. Then she suggested that I take it to my father while pretending to be Esau. I told her that even if my father couldn't see well, he could feel, and tell from my smooth arms that I wasn't Esau. She took the skins of the goats, which had been killed, and wrapped them around my arms. She got some of Esau's clothing and put it on me. Then she gave me the special meal, and I went in to my father. I said, "Father." And he said, "Who is it?" I said, "It is your son, Esau, returned from the hunt. Sit up and eat the game I have gotten for you. Then you may bless me." Not satisfied to take my brother's birthright, I now took his name, and I was about to take his blessing. My father was surprised at how quickly Esau had returned, and I assured him that his God had granted me success. You see, at that time, I had no awareness that God was my God. My father wasn't sure about my voice, so he asked to feel my hands and arms. He said, "The voice is the voice of Jacob, but the hands are the hands of Esau," for he felt the fur of the goats. Then he smelled the clothes I was wearing, and he said, "That's Esau," which says something about Esau. Then he ate the meal I had brought and he blessed me, asking his God to grant me plenty of everything and indicating that I would be lord over my brother and that any who cursed me would be cursed. With that I left, and no sooner had I gone out than Esau came in with the game my father had requested. He said, "Come, father, and eat that you may bless me." At that my father trembled and told Esau that he had already given the blessing, and that according to the custom of our people, that blessing could not be taken back. Nor could it be given again. Esau cried out bitterly, "Is he not rightly named Jacob?

For he has supplanted me these two times. He took away my birthright; and now he has taken away my blessing."

Personally, I was pleased with myself, but my brother was filled with rage. He spoke to others of killing me. My mother heard of this and advised me to leave until my brother's anger subsided. She talked my father into sending me to her brother's home in Mesopotamia, where I should find a wife among my mother's people. On that journey, traveling alone, I had a strange experience. One night as I lay on the desert sleeping, I dreamed that I saw a ladder reaching from that place to heaven. Angels were ascending and descending on the ladder, and the Lord stood above it saying, "I am the Lord, the God of Abraham, your father, and the God of Isaac; the land on which you lie, I will give to you and to your descendants; your descendants will be numerous, and behold, I am with you and will keep you wherever you go, and I will bring you back to this land, for I will not leave you until I have done that which I have spoken to you."

Now, I don't know whether it was my imagination, or the result of my mind thinking about my father's blessing, or what; but it was pretty real to me. And as I said, I was not a religious man, but I didn't want to take any chances. Maybe there was a God. Maybe there was something to the religious life. In any case, it wouldn't cost anything to put it to the test. So I made a vow, though I wasn't really intending to take it seriously. I said, "If God will be with me, and will keep me in this way that I go, and will give me bread to eat and clothing to wear so that I come again to my father's house in peace, then the Lord shall be my God, and this place shall be God's house, and of all you give me I will give back a tenth to you." What did I have to lose? I had nothing. If I lost, I would owe nothing; if I succeeded, I could own up to God's place in my life later.

I am afraid that in this regard, I was like a great many people. They have the opportunity for a valid religious experience that could change their lives, but they don't want to change, so they hold God at arm's length saying, "Not now. I'm not ready. I want to go my own way and make it on my own terms." That's what I did. I effectively put God off. What could have been a profound, life-changing experience for me was set aside, postponed. And I went on my way, still very much the same Jacob I was when I had left home; but a seed had been planted.

The next name I bore wasn't so much a proper name, as it was an attitude. I would say that during the next phase of my life I was thought of as "Becky's Boy." I thought I was being indulged as a relative, whereas I found that I was really being taken advantage of. I finally arrived in Haran, in Mesopotamia, where Laban, my mother's brother lived. The first one I met from the family was Rachel, Laban's younger daughter. My heart went out to her right away. She was beautiful. Laban also had an older daughter, Leah, but she was quite plain, and not one I would choose. Rachel ran to tell her father that a kinsman had arrived, and he rushed to greet me to make me feel welcome in his home.

At first things went very well between us, and he referred to me as Becky's Boy. I worked for him a little and received room and board in return. Then he told me that I should get paid for my work. I told him that I would like to marry his daughter, Rachel, but that I had nothing to give him as a bride-price. We made an agreement that if I worked for him for seven years, it would be the same as a bride-price. So I worked for seven years, and the time went quickly, as I anticipated marriage.

When the time was completed, a wedding date was set, and the bride was brought to me, all suitably veiled. Following the wedding celebration, I went into the bridal chamber, but it wasn't until the next morning that I discovered that my bride was Leah, the older daughter. When I complained to Laban, he simply said that in his country, the oldest daughter had to be married first. "But," he said, "Don't despair. Wait a week and I will give you Rachel also, if you will work seven more years for her." You see, he just wanted my free labor for another seven years. What else could I do? I loved Rachel and I had nothing to give an exchange for her, so I consented.

I grew to distrust and despise my uncle, Laban. As I think of it now, it is probably because he was so much like me. When the second seven years were completed, I told Laban I wanted to leave. He pleaded with me to stay, for though he had sons of his own, he felt that I had brought him prosperity. I made him a deal that I would take all the multicolored animals each year as payment for caring for his flocks and herds. It occurred to me that I would be in good position to control the breeding. Laban agreed, but then he removed all the multicolored animals from the flocks under my supervision. But I got back at him. Some of the animals were already pregnant, and they produced a few multicolored offspring. I made sure that they were prominent in the breeding process in the future, and as a result, I became very rich, while Laban became poorer.

Laban's sons became more and more angry at my success, and the situation was beginning to get ugly. So one day, when Laban and his sons were off on a round-up, I gathered up my wives, my children, my servants, and my herds and left to return to Canaan. I had lived by my wits, taking whatever opportunities came my way, and I had become very wealthy. And as far as I was concerned, Becky's Boy had done it all by himself.

The next name I was to bear came from a wholly different source; it came from God. I started out for Canaan, in a rather confident mood, surrounded by retainers and family. But the closer I got, the more realistic I became about what might lay before me. I had not thought about Esau for twenty years, but the closer I got to Canaan, the more I thought. Not that I was penitent, but I was anxious. Would Esau still be harboring a grudge? Would he try to kill all of us?

I had not thought about the God who approached me twenty years earlier either. I had been too busy getting along by whatever means I could. As we came near to the place where I had that first vision, I had a dream one night in which I saw a legion of angels. It reminded me that I had made an agreement years before, that if God would prosper me, I would acknowledge him. It had never occurred to me in all those twenty years that what I had received had anything to do with God. Now I began to wonder: Is it possible that God had been with me all the time, when I was living my life in such utter disregard for His way?

As interesting as such speculation might be, the more immediate problem at hand was the confrontation with Esau. I had manipulated other situations to my benefit; why not this one? I made up several groups of animals, and sent them on ahead, advising my servants that if anyone from the clan of Esau should ask what these animals were for, my servants were to say, "These are a gift to my Lord Esau from his brother, Jacob." I hoped that after encountering several such groups, Esau's anger might be mellowed.

At the River Jabbok, some of my returning servants met me, saying that they had met Esau, and that he was on his way to see me with 400 men. I did not know what to expect. So, for further protection, I divided my family and retinue into two groups and sent them off in slightly different directions, in the hope that, if one were harmed, the other at least might be spared.

It was that night I found myself alone by the river, awaiting the arrival of my brother the next day. That night was agony for me. My whole life passed before me, and I could see the kind of crafty, manipulating, aggressive, self-centered person I had become. I had brought my present state upon myself. Could I find forgiveness from Esau? Could I find forgiveness from God? I wrestled all that night with my conscience — one part of my nature not wishing to change; the other insisting that there had to be a change. At times, I felt I was wrestling with God himself, alternately resisting God and holding onto him, as I struggled for meaning in my mixed-up life. As dawn broke, the decision was made, and I yielded to God. I felt a profound change come over me, as though I were a different person. I felt that God was telling me, "No longer shall you be known as Jacob, 'the Supplanter.' Hereafter, you shall be called 'Israel,' meaning, 'He who strives with God.'"

It was this experience that brought home to me the reality of God's grace. Life is filled with all kinds of hurdles, and it often seems that conniving, greed, jealousy, and deceit are the only ways to survive. Believe me, they are not. They only lead to broken relationships, broken hearts, and to people who we are afraid to meet. I had tried all that, and I felt that God was far behind me, but in this experience I discovered that God is always with us, no matter who we are or what we have been, and God is always calling us to try a better way. If we trust God, we can be different people, better than we have been.

Let me close by saying that that change affected everything. I now knew that I was forgiven by God, but I still had to face Esau. As Esau and his 400 men drew nearer, I crossed the river and waited for him. When he came up to me, I bowed myself to the ground and humbly asked his forgiveness. The next thing I knew, Esau, too, was on his knees, embracing me, kissing me and calling me "brother." It could have worked out badly, but in my case it didn't. And the sweetest name I ever bore, was this last one, "brother," for it meant that I had been forgiven.

I have told you all of this to help you see that no matter what you've been, no matter what you may have done, no matter how long you've been going down the wrong path, it is possible to change, to get right with God, and to find forgiveness.

My House Will Serve the Lord: Joshua

Joshua 24:1-15, 24

Perhaps you have heard how a man named Joshua fought the battle of Jericho. The incident has been immortalized in ballad and legend. But the trouble with such immortalization is that it concentrates on the incident and overlooks the deeper meaning, or it elevates an individual but fails to give proper credit to all involved. I choose Jericho as a case in point because I was there. In fact, I *am* that Joshua about whom you may have heard.

Jericho was not important simply because we were victorious but because it signified a growing faith in my people; faith in themselves, faith in their destiny, and most of all, faith in God. That faith had been a long time in coming. It's not that they had had no faith up to that time, but their faith had often been misplaced, and as a result, they were weak. I have discovered from personal experience that a nation's strength lies in its faith. Let me share with you how faith developed among my people. Perhaps you will be able to make some application to yourself and your people.

The first thing I want to point out is the weakness that accompanies misplaced faith. Our people were camped by Mount Sinai. A few months earlier we had successfully marched out of Egypt, and for several months thereafter, we had been making our way through the desert to that place. Our ancestors had been nomads in that part of the country, but none of us, with the exception of Moses, our leader, had ever been there. We were a rag-tag band of former slaves from various tribes with nothing more to hold us together than a dimly remembered common history, and the words of this man, Moses, that the God of our ancestors had spoken to him and commanded him to deliver us from bondage.

When we arrived at Mount Sinai, Moses indicated that God was going to communicate with us. But when we heard the rumble of volcanoes and felt the movement of earthquakes — things we did not understand — we asked Moses to go up into the mountain to get the message for us. He agreed, but also chose some elders from the tribes to go part way with him. He also chose me, Joshua, son of Nun, of the tribe of Ephraim, to accompany him. I was a young man, and so I was able to go farther than the rest, but even I was not present when Moses talked with God.

For forty days, we were up on the mountain. When Moses returned to us, he had two tablets of stone on which he had written the Ten Commandments, the rules which were to bind us together and help us to live as God's people. As our small party drew nearer to the camp, we heard the sound of shouting. I said that it was the noise of war and that we should hurry to camp. Moses said that it was neither the sound of victory, nor the sound of defeat, but of singing. And sure enough, when we arrived at the camp, the people were dancing and making merry around a golden calf which, during our absence, Aaron, Moses' brother, had made of the rings and bracelets of the people. The people were worshiping the calf and suggesting that this image, which they had made, was the god that had brought them out of Egypt.

Moses was enraged. One of the commandments on his stone tablets said that we should neither make images of any gods, nor worship them, and here the people were doing just that. In anger, Moses broke the stone tablets, an act symbolic of the people's breaking of the commandment. Then he broke the golden image and ground it to dust.

I learned from this incident that people are anxious to put their faith in something, but sometimes faith is misplaced. It is incredible that anyone should worship something they have made with their own hands. And yet, that is so often what people do — they worship wealth, material objects, or people who have the same weaknesses they have, but that kind of faith can never bring out the best in them. My people had to learn to trust in a God not made with hands — a lesson people must learn in every generation.

On another occasion, we were encamped at Rephedim, not far from Sinai. While we were there, a band of nomadic marauders, the Amalekites, began to attack us. This was the first armed force we had met since leaving Egypt. If we should lose, our people would be thrown into confusion. The success of our journey to freedom depended on our repelling this attack. Yet, we had no trained military force. Moses turned to me and said, "Go among the people and choose the best men, and go and fight with the Amalekites." Suddenly, I was a military commander. I chose the best men I could find and we engaged the Amalekites in a valley. As far as my people were concerned, I was a nobody. Moses was the one they trusted, but he was now too old to lead the fight. So he climbed to the top of a mountain where he could be seen by our army, and whenever he held his arms up, our people took heart and prevailed; whenever he let his arms down, our people became apprehensive, and the Amalekites prevailed. Sensing this, two of the elders took turns holding up Moses' arms when he got weary, and as a result of this, we were successful in the battle.

Here again, the people were demonstrating faith — but it was faith in a man — Moses. If that man were not present, or if he appeared to be getting weary, the people weakened. I suppose that people are still like that: they will follow a national hero, they look for someone on whom to focus their confidence, but if that person is taken from them, they become dismayed because they have no higher allegiance to guide them. My people had to find something beyond human leadership to put their faith in.

Eventually, our wanderings brought us near the borders of the land which Moses had promised us — the land of Canaan. Moses selected a man from each of the twelve tribes to go into the land, spy it out, and bring back a report. I was selected from the tribe of Ephraim. We spent forty days exploring the land. When we returned, we brought back figs, pomegranates, and an enormous cluster of grapes to show our people the fertility of the land. After our many months on the desert, it really did seem that Canaan was a land flowing with milk and honey.

But most of the spies had been more impressed with the strength of the people and the fortification of their cities, rather than with the goodness of the land. Ten of them advised against going in. Only Caleb and I were confident that God would be with us. Our people were in an uproar. They spoke against Moses and they threatened to stone Caleb and me. They talked of choosing a new captain who would lead them back to the security of slavery in Egypt. It was obvious that they were simply not ready to enter the promised land. They had been slaves too long, and it was not likely that those people would ever change.

So Moses stood up and told the people that since they were not willing to go in and take the land, they simply would not be allowed to go in. Only two people of that generation, he said, who had had enough faith to believe that God would be with them, namely Caleb and I, would be allowed to enter. Moses then said that for every day the spies had spent in searching out the land, the people would spend a year wandering in the wilderness. In other words, it would be forty years before they would get another chance. The present generation would be dead, and a whole new generation that had not known slavery, would be born. The people protested. They pleaded to enter. Some even tried to go in without Moses, but they had no real confidence, and they were defeated. So we set out for the wilderness once again, waiting for forty years to pass.

I learned from this experience that it is difficult for some people to have faith in the future. They are so enslaved by the past that they can only think of the "good old days," no matter how bad those days may have been. The root of the problem is lack of faith in God. They want only a sure thing. Everything has to be laid out before them in such a way that doesn't require any faith at all to move ahead. If they can't have that kind of guarantee in advance, they refuse to move ahead. They have no confidence that the God who has sustained them thus far, will continue to sustain them. Such people miss most of the good things that God has in store for them, as my people missed their chance to enter the promised land.

The remainder of my story is, fortunately, the happier part. Our people did wander as nomads from place to place through the wilderness areas of Sinai for forty years. But as we wandered, we were gaining strength. We were growing in numbers. We were getting accustomed to the area. A new generation, which prized freedom and independence, was growing up. We were learning about the God who called us out of Egypt, and we had a clearer picture of what it meant to be God's people. Moreover, we were developing a sense of national identity, a sense of destiny, a growing confidence in God and in ourselves.

When it became apparent to Moses that we were ready to enter the promised land, he called all the people together. He informed them that he was now too old to lead the people into the promised land, but that God had instructed him to choose a successor whom the people should follow. Then, in the presence of the people, Moses laid his hands on me and commissioned me to lead the people. Soon after that, Moses climbed up to the heights of Mount Pisgah, where he could look across the Jordan River and see the promised land, and up there on that mountaintop, he died.

After a period of mourning for Moses, my people were ready to move. No longer were there expressions of fear or negative comments. The people had become a disciplined force who trusted in God and believed in their destiny. It was the time of the harvest, the time when the Jordan overflows its banks, making the river impassable, even at the fords. The people were not dismayed; they simply asked for direction. I organized them by companies and placed twelve priests carrying the Ark of the Covenant, our symbol of God's presence, out in front. I told the priests that when they got to the edge of the river they should just keep on going, and God would see that we got across. You may not believe this, but when the priests entered the edge of the river, the water stopped flowing! Some people have pointed out that landslides upstream have been known to block the Jordan for considerable periods of time. Perhaps that is what happened, I don't know. It doesn't much matter to me *how* it was accomplished, I am only interested in the fact that it *was* accomplished.

I am telling you this, not to get you to believe in a miracle, but to show you that if great things are to be accomplished, people sometimes have to step out in faith. In fact, for most of us, the future opens up only one step at a time.

Before we could go farther, we needed to know what we were up against, so, as Moses had done before me, I sent out spies. This time, I sent only two. They were to look over the city of Jericho, observe its fortifications, estimate its available manpower, and find a way to capture it. When they arrived at the city, they went to the house of a harlot named Rahab. No one would pay any attention to two strange men coming and going from such a place, they reasoned. Rahab, apparently, had no affection for the people among whom she was living, and as might be expected, she was a gold mine of information.

When the ruler of the place learned of the presence of strangers in the city, he sought them out, but Rahab hid them, and let them down from a back window, as she happened to live on the city wall. She only asked that she and her family be spared in the coming conflict. The spies returned and told us that the inhabitants of Jericho feared us, and that the city would be easy to take.

We were convinced that God was with us. Perhaps that is a mistaken notion; perhaps, as God of the universe, God is really with all people. But at that time, we still had much to learn about God. We conceived of him as *our* God exclusively, therefore, our enemies were thought to be God's enemies. God may be the God of all people, but at the time, we alone recognized God; we alone had agreed to serve God and be God's people.

Before we attacked Jericho, we marched around the city for six days, out of arrow shot, carrying the Ark of the Covenant, no one speaking a word. That in itself, must have unsettled the inhabitants. On the seventh day, we marched around seven times while the priests blew loudly on their trumpets. At the end of our seventh march that day, the priests gave a loud blast on the trumpets and before our eyes sections of the wall began to crumble and fall! Conquest of the city was easy. Some people have said that it was nothing more than a well-timed earthquake. Again, I don't choose to argue about *how* it happened — I can only report that it *happened*, and that it confirmed our faith in our destiny. We were destined to have a land of our own, and we were convinced that God was helping us to get it. I realize that my telling of the story is colored by our supposition that God was uniquely interested in us.

From that initial victory at Jericho, we moved forward, and eventually occupied most of the land of Canaan, dividing it among our tribes. But what concerned me the most was whether the people would remain faithful to the covenant that they made with God, which made them a unique people. After the land was settled, I called for an assembly of all the tribes of Israel at Shechem. I reminded them of their ancestors, of all they had been through as a people, and of the wonderful ways in which God had sustained them during all those difficult years. I told them that the only thing that made us different from the peoples who surrounded us was that we acknowledged God and had committed ourselves to God. I said, "Choose this day whom you will serve... as for me and my house, we will serve the Lord." My people answered, as with one voice, "The Lord our God we will serve, and his voice, we will obey." Now, my question to you is, "How about you? Who do you serve? Whose voice do you obey?" That is something that only you can decide.

The Sword of the Lord: Gideon

Judges 6:11-18

How does a man help his nation when his people are de-moralized, his land is occupied by the enemy, and there is no one to unite his people and give them hope? That question used to trouble me a lot, until one day I began to get some answers. My name is Gideon, son of Joash, of the clan of the Abiezrites, of the tribe of Manasseh. When my people settled in the land of Palestine, they gave up their nomadic ways to become farmers. But there were other nomadic peoples who made it a practice to prey on farmers and take for themselves the fruit of our labors.

In my day, the invaders were the Midianites, a people of the desert. Each year at harvest time, they would move in from the desert with their camels, flocks, and herds and armies and cover the land like a plague of locusts. My people were weak and disunited and had no means of protecting themselves. All we could do was to hide in caves and mountain hideouts, hoping to escape with our lives, until the Midianites had used up the grain and decided to move on. My people cried to the Lord for deliverance, but the only help we received was a wandering prophet who went about reminding us that a long time ago, when our people were in bondage in Egypt, God had delivered us, and we had promised to be faithful to God. He pointed out that at the moment we were not being very faithful, for we were worshiping other gods, and it was this absence of faithfulness that was responsible for our plight. A lot of good that preaching did us! We needed weapons, not words; a general, not a prophet. But the prophet was all we were sent.

It was then that I began having some experiences that changed my life and the life of my people. I would like to share my discoveries with you.

Perhaps the first thing I should mention is my discovery that God is present in the ordinary routine of life. I was busy one day threshing wheat in the secrecy of a wine press. Believe me, that's no easy task! We were accustomed to threshing wheat out in the open, using our oxen to trample the grain, but with the Midianites in the land, we had to work in secret, doing the work by hand, lest the Midianites discover the grain and take it for themselves. As I was beating out the grain, I was talking to myself about the sorry state of my people, and thinking about those discomforting words of the prophet.

I looked up for a moment, and there was a man sitting under an oak tree, watching me. At least I think it was a man. At any rate, he claimed to be a messenger from God, who said to me, "The Lord is with you, you mighty warrior." I looked at him and said sarcastically, "Pray, sir, if the Lord is with us, then why has all this befallen us? And where are all those wonderful deeds that our forefathers recounted to us, saying, 'Didn't the Lord bring us up from Egypt? But now the Lord has cast us off and given us into the hands of the Midianites.' The man then said to me, 'Go in this might of yours to deliver Israel from the hand of Midian; do not I send you?' I responded, 'How can I deliver Israel? My clan is the weakest in our tribe, and I the least in my family.' But the man said, 'God will be with you.' "

This was pretty strong talk. My head was spinning. I don't know whether the man was really there, or whether I was talking to myself, or whether God was talking to me face-to-face. I do know that it was a religious experience and the turning point in my life. I felt that God had sought me out, not in my place of worship, but in my work. He had spoken to me, not before an altar, but through my thoughts, or perhaps it was through conversation with another person. I got the distinct understanding that any activity on the part of God was going to come about through human instruments. God had used a prophet to get me thinking: a man to challenge me, who said God would use me to deliver Israel, if I would let him.

Any of us who are looking for God to be active in history had better get used to the idea that when God acts, he acts through us, and the more open we are to his direction by earnestly seeking his guidance, the more useful we will be.

Another thing I learned is that people have to decide what is central to their lives and to commit themselves to it. Most of our people were acquainted with the name of God, but in practice, they were pagan. They needed to have it brought home to them that they would never be any stronger than that to which they were committed. It so happened that most of them worshiped at the altar of Baal, the god of the land, whose worship we had taken over from the Canaanites who lived in the land before we arrived.

I felt an irresistible urge to pull down the altar of Baal and to erect a new altar for the worship of the living God. Under cover of night, I went with ten of my hired hands and tore down the altar of Baal and the image that was next to it, and I made a new altar to God. When the men of the village awoke the next morning and saw what had been done, they inquired who had done it. Their search led them to me. They came to the house of my father, Joash, and demanded that I be brought out and put to death for my sacrilege. My father, who had himself been a worshiper of Baal up to this point, said to the men, "Will you contend for Baal? If Baal is god, let him contend for himself, since it was his altar that was pulled down." The villagers murmured but accepted his wisdom, and when nothing happened to me, they began to see the weakness of their god.

Surely, the situation is the same in your day. People talk about God being the source of life, but in practice they follow after gods which are unable to give meaning, order, or direction to their lives. They need someone who is committed to the living God to show them the uselessness of their present pursuits, and to help them find the direction that will liberate their lives and bring them to fulfillment. That person may be you.

The next thing I had to learn was to depend on God. The Midianites once again invaded our land. I felt called to lead my people. I blew the trumpet, which called my clan together, and I sent messengers among the neighboring tribes inviting them to join us. In all, 32,000 men responded to the call. It was a sizable army, but the army of the Midianites was 135,000 men.

I wanted to be sure that I was doing the right thing, so I devised a test. I put out a sheepskin on a threshing floor, and I said to God, "If in the morning the fleece is wet with dew, and all the ground is dry, I will know that you will deliver Israel by my hand." The next morning the fleece was wet, and the ground was dry. Still, it was a big decision, so I put out the fleece again the next night and said to God, "If the fleece is dry, and the ground is wet, then I will know that you are with us." The next morning, the fleece was dry and the ground was wet. I don't say that that is the way everyone should determine God's will, but it worked for me. I will say, however, that our decisions should be subject to periodic testing, so that we don't get too far ahead, without taking the opportunity to correct our course.

With this new confidence, I led my people to a place where the Midianites were camped. Then God spoke to me and said, "The people with you are too many. When the victory comes to them, they will say they have delivered themselves because of the size of their army. Therefore, tell the people that whoever is fearful may return home." I made the offer, and 22,000 returned to their homes! We were now trimmed down to an army of 10,000, and I was beginning to get pretty apprehensive. Then God spoke to me again and said, "The people are still too many. Take them to the river to drink and keep only those men who lift up the water to drink from their hands." I thought that was a good idea, for the most alert troops would drink that way. But I was dismayed to discover that only 300 of my men drank that way! Nevertheless, I kept these men and dismissed the rest. You can be sure that there was great murmuring now among the remaining troops, and I myself was unsure about the decision. I understood that a victory based on our own strength would carry Israel farther from God, but this kind of weakness, 300 men against 135,000, was unthinkable.

Nevertheless, I went down to reconnoiter the enemy camp under cover of darkness. While I was there, hidden in the underbrush, I heard one enemy sentry tell another of a dream that he had had. The dream spoke of the great fear the Midianites had of me and of my army. Psychologically, the Midianites were ill prepared to fight us, in spite of their great numbers, and it was on the basis of this fear that I devised my plan.

I saw to it that each of my men had a trumpet and a jar with a lighted torch inside that could not be seen. Then I arranged my 300 men on the hills around the perimeter of the Midianites. When it was dark, at a command from me, each man blew his trumpet, broke the jar so that the torch burst into flame, and shouted, "A sword for the Lord and for Gideon." The noise and the torches set the Midianites in such disarray that they ran into each others' weapons, stampeded their own animals, and thousands of them were killed by their own men in the ensuing confusion. The remainder fled and were pursued by us and by other men from the tribes of Israel. From that time on the Midianites never again were a problem to the people of Israel.

What I want to get across is that the victory was really God's victory. You can call it psychological warfare, or superior strategy, or what have you, but 300 men would never have been able to overthrow such a formidable foe without the help that came from God. That help was in the form of a unifying faith, a conviction that God can and does act through people, the belief that there is a moral order in the universe that ultimately supports justice and righteousness, and a willingness to trust in the rightness of our cause, rather than in the size of our army.

These are lessons from my experience that I believe can benefit every nation and person, in your day or in mine. I must confess that I thought at the time God was just naturally on the side of Israel and opposed to Midian. I no longer believe that. I don't think that God is on the side of any one nation to the exclusion of another. All people are God's children, and God is distressed by the destruction of any. But I do believe that it is necessary for an individual, as well as for a nation, to choose to side with God by choosing uprightness and justice. The nation or person that is indifferent to justice and uprightness may temporarily succeed, as did the Midianites, but they will ultimately fail. The nation or person that practices justice and uprightness may, of course, have its share of difficulties, but I am confident that ultimately their cause will prosper. May justice and uprightness be the course you choose, individually and as a nation.

The Outsider:
Ruth and Boaz

Ruth 1:16-18

In the old days of Israel, when the people of Israel came out of Egypt and wanted to enter the land of Palestine in order to settle it as their promised land, it was necessary for them to pass through territory that was held by other people. The Israelites said they simply wanted peaceful passage, but those who held the surrounding territories were often afraid, suspicious, or hostile. Among such people were the Moabites, who did everything they could, including the hiring of a sorcerer, to keep the people of Israel from passing through their land.

The people of Israel did manage to get through, however, and when they became settled in the land of Palestine, they did not forget the hostility of the people of Moab. Though they were not at war with each other, each group did look down on the other, and many of the people of Israel, even centuries later, felt that there was no place for a Moabite, either among the people of Israel, or even in the providence of God. There were those who said that the Jews must not marry Moabites, or that if a Jew had already married a Moabite, they should divorce.

The experiences that I want to share are just the opposite of that. I'm here to speak *against* the idea that God is exclusively the God of one people as opposed to another. I think that the story that I have to tell shows that God is not concerned with race or nation. Rather, I believe, that all people stand equally before him. I am one of those men you seldom hear of, except when referred to as the husband of a more famous woman. My name is Boaz; the name of my wife is Ruth. I have to go back in time to begin our story.

daughter-in-law of the widowed Naomi. I remembered then that I had heard that Naomi had returned with a daughter-in-law, who had forsaken her land and people in order to look after Naomi. I recognized too that she was part of a family that was related to me, so I went to her and urged her to glean only in my fields, and to stay near my men, who would protect her, for as a foreigner she had little protection from the law. She bowed humbly before me and asked why I would be concerned for the welfare of a foreigner. I told her that I had heard of what she was doing for her mother-in-law, and I said I was sure that the God of Israel would grant her refuge and protection. At lunchtime, I invited her to eat with me, and I noticed how she saved some food to be taken home to Naomi. Subsequently, I told my men to leave generous amounts of grain, where it would be easy for her to gather it.

When Ruth went home that day, she must have told Naomi all that happened, because neighbors said that for the first time in a long time, Naomi was able to praise God. Apparently, she could see the hand of God in what was taking place. Each day, Ruth came to glean in my fields, and I found myself thinking more and more about her sterling qualities.

As time went on, Naomi became increasingly concerned that Ruth should have a husband, so that Naomi herself could have heirs. I didn't know it then, but Naomi had already decided that I was the logical husband for her daughter-in-law. I guess she thought I was moving too slowly, however, so she decided to prod me into action. She laid a plan, which was designed to move things one way or the other. One night, while I was sleeping at the threshing floor with my men, as we guarded the grain from theft, Ruth came at Naomi's direction, and laid down by me. Since I was surrounded by other men, her reputation was at stake. I awoke, startled to discover her there, and when I asked her what she was doing there, she said, in effect, "You are my kinsman, and I need your protection." For the first time I saw just how vulnerable she was, and how much she really did need someone to protect her. She had put herself in a position where I could either take *advantage* of her or take *responsibility* for her. Confronted with that moment of decision, I discovered that I loved her, and that I was willing to take responsibility for her.

But it was not so simple. We have a custom among our people called Levirate marriage. That means that if a man dies without leaving heirs, it is up to his brother to marry the widow. The first child born of such a union would be acknowledged as a child of the deceased husband and be entitled to the estate of the deceased. You will recall that Ruth's husband had a brother, but he too was dead, so the right of Levirate marriage would go to the nearest next of kin and there was a relative nearer than I.

I sent Ruth back to Naomi, and the next morning, I called that nearer relative before the elders of the village to see whether he wished to exercise his right. First, I told him that there was a family property up for sale, and that he had the first option to buy it. That was true, because without a man to care for the land, Naomi would have to sell what she had. To my disappointment, he said he was interested and would redeem the property. I then informed him that there was also a childless widow who went with the property and that he would have to marry her. When he thought of the inheritance complication, and that the land would not stay in his family, he decided to forfeit his right and turn it over to me.

I immediately purchased the property and announced my intention to marry Ruth. We were soon married, and eventually had a son, who was recognized as Naomi's heir. As a result, Naomi's life was fulfilled, Ruth was provided for, and I found a fine wife. But there is more. The child who was born to us we named Obed. In time, he married and had a son, who was named Jesse. And in his time, Jesse had a son, whose name was David, the greatest of Israel's kings.

And generations later there was born in David's line, in the same city of Bethlehem, Jesus, whom Christians call Lord and Savior.

The whole point of my story is this: If God saw fit to include a foreigner in the blood line of Israel's greatest king, and of the Messiah himself, then there is no room in the plan of God for racial prejudice or national prejudice. None of us has anything of which to boast, not race, not religion, not privileged circumstances, for we are equally loved. All of us are the children of our heavenly Father. We are all part of God's family and that is how we must treat one another.

The Sweet Singer of Israel: David

Psalm 23

My name is David, son of Jesse, of the village of Bethlehem, of the tribe of Judah. By the grace of God, I was chosen to be king over the kingdoms of Judah and Israel. As a result of my experiences, I feel I have much to share, which may be helpful to you, if you don't mind listening to an old man.

The first thing I want to tell you about is my youth. I was the youngest of eight children to be born to my father. Being the youngest, it fell to me to watch over my father's sheep. This meant that I was out in the open a great deal, and, while I dreamed then about the imagined excitement of city life, I now know what a great opportunity it was for me to spend my early years out in the open. Those long hours in the shade of a tree gave me opportunities to behold the handiwork of the Creator. I took my harp along and learned to play uninhibited by my mistakes. I composed songs using the imagery of the pastoral scene around me: the abundance of God's provision, the green pastures, the still waters, the restoration that comes from a cool drink, the valley of the dark shadows, the nearness of God in all his creation. Here I had time for contemplation that life in the city would never have afforded me. I think that God often uses nature to speak to us, if we will just pay attention. That thought is lifted up in one of the songs that we Hebrews used in our worship: "I lift up my eyes to the hills. From whence does my help come? My help comes from the Lord, who made heaven and earth" (Psalm 121:1-2).

There is another experience from my youth that stands out in my mind. One day, Samuel, the prophet of God who represented the voice of God to us, came to our home. I was

your vindication shine like the light, and the justification of your cause like the noonday" (Psalm 37:5-6).

Following my victory over Goliath, I became a popular hero, and Saul subsequently made me one of the commanders in his army. Eventually, he even gave me his daughter in marriage. It seemed that everything was going along just fine for me, but Saul was a moody person, subject to severe depressions. I used to play the harp for him to bring him out of those depressions and to soothe his anger. On more than one occasion he felt so persecuted that he threw his spear at me as I tried to soothe him. I tried to help him on the battlefield, too, scoring victories over the enemy, but even here I ran into trouble, for when we would return from the campaign, people would rush up to us and shout, "Saul has slain his thousands, and David his tens of thousands." This did nothing to help our relationship.

Saul felt the kingdom slipping from him, and he blamed me. His anger and jealousy became so violent that I had to flee for my life. I was forced to live in the wilderness, fleeing from place to place before the relentless pursuit of the king. I, who only recently had been a general, I who had lived in the king's house as his son-in-law, I, who sensed a destiny to be the king in Israel, was now a fugitive, an outlaw. I penned some thoughts on those difficult times: "This poor man cried, and the Lord heard him, and saved him out of all his troubles... O taste and see that the Lord is good! Happy are those who take refuge in him" (Psalm 34:8).

Others, who were debtors or malcontents, or otherwise in distress, came to me, and I became a commander of a small army of refugees. We managed to survive but only because we lived by our wits. On occasions, I could have killed the king, but I was sure that it was not God's will that I should come to the throne by murder. The time came when Saul died in battle, and the people of my own tribe, Judah, selected me to be their king. Seven years later, all the other tribes of Israel did the same, and I became ruler of the two kingdoms, Judah and Israel. Even when I was being pursued, I was confident that the Lord would deliver me. Listen to these words that I composed as I hid out from King Saul: "The Lord is my rock, my fortress, and my deliverer, my God, my rock in whom I take refuge, my shield, and the horn of my salvation, my stronghold. I call upon the Lord, who is worthy to be praised, and I am saved from my enemies" (Psalm 18:2-3).

Following my accession to both thrones, I was successful in taking the fortress of Jerusalem from the Jebusites, and there I set up the capitol of my kingdom. I had been a soldier most of my life, and I knew the importance of discipline for myself, as well as for my troops. All of my time and energy had been directed to getting to this place, but now that I had arrived, there were changes in my attitude that I had not expected. The enemy was subdued; I had met victory after victory; my kingdom was expanding and my position was secure. For the first time, I was in a position to send others out to the battlefield, while I stayed at Jerusalem, and occupied myself with other thoughts. I began to feel that there was nothing in the whole world that would be denied me, if I but desired it, and this was the beginning of the hardest lesson I was ever to learn: the importance of self-discipline.

I'm not proud of what I'm about to tell you; indeed, it is hard for me to speak of it, but if you listen to it, perhaps you can profit from my experience. It began one day when I had arisen from my midday nap. I was looking down from the roof of my palace, when I chanced to see a young woman bathing on the rooftop of a building not far away. My instincts seized me, and I was consumed with desire for her. I went to inquire who she was, and I discovered that her name was Bathsheba, wife of Uriah the Hittite, one of my warriors, who was at that moment on the battlefield. I requested her presence and she was obligated to come. As king, my power was absolute in the kingdom, and no one questioned my conduct or decisions. A relationship developed between us, fed by my passion and her submission, and before long, she was with child.

Hoping to cover what had been done, before the scandal became common knowledge, I called her husband from the battlefield on the pretext of asking for a battle report. My hope was that he would spend a few nights at home and thereby cover the deed. But he was more of a man than I. He refused to go to his wife or to his home while his men were living in jeopardy on the battlefield. I was angered by his integrity, for it was in contrast to my own, and in anger I wrote a secret order to his commander to put Uriah in the forefront of the battle, and then to withdraw from him so that he would be killed. Soon after, I received word that Uriah had been killed in battle.

After an appropriate time of mourning, Bathsheba and I were married, and she moved into the palace. I tried to occupy myself with affairs of state; I tried to lose myself in work; I tried to forget what I had done, but to no avail. I have been a religious person all my life, and what I had done was against all my training. Still, we often do things that are against our training and against our consciences; in the heat of passion we take what we want, and then we find that we are more unhappy than before because we carry around the burden of guilt.

I was in such a state, when one day, Nathan, the prophet of God, and my longtime friend, came to me. He had a case for me to judge. There was a poor man, he said, who had just one lamb that he kept as a family pet. The lamb ate and slept with the members of the family, and was dear to all of them. The poor man worked for a wealthy landowner, who had great flocks and herds. One day a guest was to come and visit the wealthy man, and, instead of preparing a feast from his own flocks and herds, the rich man had taken the poor man's only lamb. When I heard the story, I was enraged. I grabbed my sword and said, "Who is this man? He doesn't deserve to live!" At that point, Nathan pointed his finger at me and said, "You are the man!" He cut me to the quick. At once I saw his point, and I fell to my knees to confess my sins. On that occasion, I wrote a prayer of confession: "Have mercy on me, O God, according to your steadfast love; according to your abundant mercy, blot out my transgressions. Wash me thoroughly from my iniquity and cleanse me from my sin" (Psalm 51:1-2).

Nathan listened, and he assured me that since I had acknowledged my guilt, God would forgive my sins. The weight of the guilt fell from me as though a heavy burden had suddenly been dropped. Now mark this: I was forgiven, but the situation could never again be as though these things had never happened. There were consequences, and they were staggering. My children were well aware of my lawless acts, and they learned far more from observing my actions than from listening to my words. My son, Amnon, seduced his sister; Absolom, another son, killed Amnon and ran away; Absolom, my favorite, later rose up in rebellion and almost took the kingdom from me by force; and Absolom himself was subsequently killed. These things were set in motion by my own undisciplined passion and violence.

Long life and experience with authority have led me to conclude that no one can do just as he pleases, not even the ruler. We are all dependent upon one another, the governed, and those who govern. The only way to have a peaceful society is to govern in justice and fairness. Reflecting on the meaning of authority caused me to write some words for my heirs, who would follow me on the throne: "When one rules justly over men, ruling in the fear of God, he dawns on them like the morning light, like the sun shining forth upon a cloudless morning, like rain that makes grass to sprout

Take my own situation: I felt it was important to challenge Baal, so I challenged him at the foundation of his supposed authority, control of the weather. I appeared before King Ahab and said: "As the Lord, the God of Israel lives, before whom I stand, there shall be neither dew nor rain these years, except by my word." I was confident that my God, the maker of heaven and earth, had put it into my heart to utter this warning, and thereby to make it absolutely clear who was in control of the universe. Apparently, the king did not take me very seriously at first, for he made no attempt to detain me.

Nevertheless, I fled from his presence and went into the wilderness. I stayed by the brook Cerith so as to have water during the drought. The ravens came there to drink, and it was from their food that I had enough to survive. It was during those long days in the wilderness that I had opportunity to think about my situation, and I began to feel sorry for myself. I had faithfully followed the command of God and delivered his message, and this was my reward: to live as a fugitive in the wilderness.

In time, however, it occurred to me that perhaps God was using the occasion to teach me, as well as Ahab, that we do God's bidding not because we are rewarded for it, but because this is what we must do when we are God's servants. Our reward is not in personal gain, but in being chosen to serve. I was not outwardly rewarded, but at least, I was provided for — or so I thought, until the brook dried up from the drought that I had predicted. Again, I began to feel sorry for myself, until I realized that this was God's way of getting me to move on.

Each of us needs to be more aware of the doors that open and close in our lives. Sometimes, our worst experiences give us the best guidance. I have discovered that God directs us more often by circumstances than by a clear word. I didn't know it then, but he was giving me my next assignment.

I had to leave the brook. I could not be seen in Israel, so I went to the territory of Sidon and came to a town called Zarephath. As I entered the village, I saw a woman, a widow, gathering a few sticks for a fire. I was hungry, and I said, "Please bring me something to eat." She reminded me that there was a drought, and she said that she had just enough flour and oil to bake some bread for herself and for her son, and after that she expected to die. She was in bad shape; she needed something to give her the will to live, some confidence that life was worth living. So I told her, "Prepare something for me first, then for yourselves, and there will be enough." I don't know whether she believed me or not. She may have felt that the situation was so hopeless anyway, that she had little to lose. In any case, she served me first, and she found that she did have enough for her son and for herself for that day. I looked her in the eyes and said, "The jar of meal shall not be empty and cruse of oil shall not fail, until the day that the Lord sends rain upon the earth." Somehow, my confidence gave her new faith, and each day we found enough provisions to see us through. I believe she learned that when we share, we are blessed.

I learned something too. While I had been staying by the brook Cerith, my constant focus had been on how to save my own life. I had been led away from that problem by having my focus changed to saving the life of another person, and of restoring her faith. That is why I say that we often discover God's will in unpleasant experiences. I also found that doing God's will, once we have discovered it, is not necessarily the easy way, but if we are committed to the service of God, there can be no other way.

The second point I want to make is that if we are going to please God, we have to make a definite decision to follow him. This is what I wanted to get across to my people, Israel.

So it was that, when the time seemed right, I left Zarephath and went to see the king. I found him out in the countryside, looking for grass for his cavalry horses. I was glad he was not in the palace with Jezebel, for she was more dangerous than he. When we met, he said, "Is it you, you troubler of Israel?" How often it is the person who sees an evil and cries out against it who is called the disturber of the peace, when it is the actions of others that are responsible for the circumstances. A prophet does not create situations of good or evil, he simply points out that because certain actions have been taken, certain results will follow. So I told him that it was not I who troubled Israel, but he who had forsaken God and followed Baal.

I told the king that if he wanted to end the drought, he should call all the people of Israel to gather on Mount Carmel, and all the prophets of Baal as well. You may be sure that he took me seriously this time.

On the agreed-upon day there was a great assemblage on the mountain. I came among the people of Israel and I said, "How long will you go limping with two different opinions? If the Lord is God, follow him; but if Baal, then follow him." The people were silent, some from shame, others from fear of the king. So I offered a contest: Let the 450 prophets of Baal build an altar to their god, lay wood upon it, and place their sacrifice upon it, and I would do likewise for my God. Let them call on the name of their god. And I would call on the name of my God; and whichever god answers by fire, let him be God. The people said that that was a good idea. I don't know how the prophets of Baal felt, but they were forced into a showdown and they accepted.

I let the 450 prophets do their work first. It was a sight to behold: They prepared their altar, and then began to chant, "O Baal, answer us!" There was no voice, no answer. Then they began limping around the altar on one foot and then the other. I urged them on: "Cry louder, perhaps he is thinking, or is gone aside, or is on the journey. Perhaps he is asleep.

They cried louder and became more frenzied. They raved on, but there was no voice; no one answered; no one heeded.

When they had had their time, I picked up the stones that had previously been used as an altar to God, and with them I rebuilt the altar of the Lord. It was a symbol that what had previously been Israel's glory, her trust in God, must be restored. I prepared the wood for the sacrifice; then I poured twelve buckets of water on it, to symbolize the rain that we sought. Actually, I didn't know what to do next, but there was no turning back now, so I prayed, "O, Lord, God of Abraham, Isaac, and Israel, let it be known this day that you are God in Israel, and that I am your servant, and that I have done all these things at your word." No sooner had I spoken than the fire of the Lord fell and consumed the offering, the wood, the stones, the water, and all. You may be skeptical, but I tell you that if you had been there, you would have been convinced. Say it was lightning — I'll agree with you, it probably was — but it happened so beautifully on schedule that chance was out of the question. When the people saw it, they fell on their faces saying, "The Lord is God; the Lord is God." God had revealed himself and the people saw the necessity of making a decision. It wasn't long before we had rain aplenty.

Now, I haven't told you this to urge you to resort to magic or to teach you that God will do our bidding whenever we speak in God's name. Most of us know from experience that kind of thing just doesn't happen. My experience in that situation was unique. I was up against an impossible situation, and I just had to act on faith that I was within the will of God. Besides, I felt strongly that I was being led by God in that matter.

What is important is not the contest, but Israel's reaction. The people were sufficiently moved that they made a decision for God, and that is the place to which all of us must come. It is not enough to remain non-committal and to say that we are keeping an open mind. It is one thing to be tolerant; it is another to be indifferent. Every person, every nation, comes to moments of decision; to defer those decisions is to undermine the moral foundations of life. We are called to commit ourselves to the highest we know, and then to live our lives by that commitment. Let me challenge you, as I did my countrymen: "If the Lord is God, then follow him." Half-hearted worship is an insult to God.

Now the third thing I want to do is to warn you that when you once commit your way to God, you must trust him. I learned that lesson the hard way. Following the defeat of the prophets of Baal, Ahab got into his chariot and raced off to tell Jezebel what had happened. Far from making a believer out of Jezebel, the news sent her into a rage, and she vowed to take my life if it were the last thing she ever did. When I heard that, I lost my nerve. I felt as though God had used me for his purpose, and now I was on my own against Jezebel. I felt as though I had given all there was to give, and the evil forces were still not won over. What was the use of further struggle?

I am ashamed to say it, but I ran away. I went to Judah in the south, all the while complaining to God that the victory had been far from complete. I had tried to stand against evil, as had the prophets before me, and I was no more successful than they had been. Jezebel lived and all her evil was arrayed against me.

One evening, I lay down under a juniper tree, and as I slept, I dreamed that angels were providing food for me, and telling me to eat so that I would be strong enough for the journey. I'm sure now that God was trying to show me that he would provide strength for my needs, and that he wanted me to go back to Israel and stand up against Jezebel, but at the time, I was so filled with fear and despair that I did not understand the dream, and I continued to press toward the south. Finally, I came to Horeb, the mountain of God, in the

Sinai Desert, where Moses had received the commandments from God. I found a cave in the side of the mountain and there I stayed, nursing my discontent. I thought, "Let God speak to me now as he did to Moses on this mountain; let me hear his voice with the clarity with which Moses heard it, and when I am made confident by such undeniable evidence as Moses found, then I will be ready to serve again." You see, I was telling God, "I want a mountaintop experience every time I am defeated or depressed." I wanted to be convinced all over again.

Let me tell you, I did have a significant experience up on that holy mountain. I fasted for forty days as had Moses, I heard the howling of the wind as had Moses, I felt the rumble of the earthquake as had Moses, I saw the fire of lightning in the heavens as did Moses. But in all this, I discovered no word from the Lord.

It was then that a strange thing happened. In the utter stillness of the desert after a storm, I heard a still, small voice — inside of me or outside of me, I do not know — but I believe that it was God who was speaking. The voice said, quite simply, "What are you doing here, Elijah?" I sputtered all kinds of excuses about how the queen sought my life, and about the importance of preserving my life, since I was probably the only person left who had not bowed to Baal. It all sounded so foolish, so self-centered, that even as I spoke, I recognized that no argument from God's side was necessary. God simply said, "Go back to where you have been. I have work yet for you to do. You are not the only one left in Israel who has not bowed to Baal. I have 7,000 who have been loyal to me." I could say nothing more. God had stopped my arguments. I was ashamed that I had not trusted more.

What I want to get across to you is the necessity of continuing to trust in God, once you have committed yourself to him. The way may not be easy, but God does not desert us; God lives, and God is ever with us. That is what I learned on Mount Horeb: God is not to be sought in holy places or in distant shrines or in the blustering forces of nature. We do not have to go to some special place to find God, God is with us where we are. God is heard in the still, small voice that speaks when we will quiet ourselves and listen. We may fail God, but God does not desert us.

Sometimes, we are tempted to think that we are the only ones left who care for decency and right. That is pride within us, and we need to humbly recognize that God is interested in these things too, and that he has others besides ourselves, who are loyal to him. You see, my pride made me think that I was all alone and that caused me to become weak and afraid. Perhaps you, too, have experienced that same discouragement I felt. Perhaps you, too, have withdrawn to the sidelines in the fight for right. Perhaps you, too, need to hear that still, small voice of God saying, "What are you doing here? Get up and get back in the fight. I have work for you to do."

Dare to Be a Daniel:
Daniel

Daniel 5:1-5, 24-28

In the year 175 BC Antiochus Epiphanes became king of the land that eventually was to be called Syria. As his kingdom was part of the area that had been conquered by Alexander the Great, he felt that it was his mission to continue to impose Greek culture on the lives of all his subjects. As he exerted this Greek influence in Palestine, there were some Jews who welcomed it and sought to profit by it. Others saw it as a threat to all that was distinctly Jewish, and they refused to have any contact with Greek ways. The stage was being set for a bloody confrontation.

At that time, I happened to be living in the city of Jerusalem, and I wanted to help my people. My name is unimportant, you wouldn't know me if I told it to you. But there is something I did that you might know about: I wrote the book of Daniel in the Old Testament. You see, this beast, Antiochus, was calling for all people to have one religion, one law, and one set of customs. Therefore, he sought to destroy Judaism. To accomplish that he placed restrictions on the observance of the sabbath; he made it illegal to practice circumcision, the mark of entrance into the Jewish faith; he required Jews to be put to death, if they were found in possession of a copy of the scriptures; he required Jews to participate in pagan festivals on pain of death if they should refuse.

It was obvious that if something was not done soon, either there would be no more Jews, or every Jew would have compromised himself to the point of shame. I was one person, I couldn't stand against the whole Syrian army. But there was one thing I could do: I could try to bring hope and courage to my people by giving them a national hero and urging them to put their trust in God.

I did not choose to write a political document urging the overthrow of Antiochus or to write anything outwardly seditious. Instead, I chose to write an allegory that might bring hope and comfort. For my hero, I reached back into the literature of my people, and selected a little-known, pious Jew, who had faced a situation similar to our own, several hundred years earlier. His name was Daniel, meaning "God has judged," an appropriate name for one who would talk about the inevitable judgment of God. There were already a number of stories about him in existence, and I pieced them together and shaped them to suit my purpose. To an outsider, they appeared to be just stories, but the oppressed people of my day would immediately make the connection and see the relevance of Daniel's experiences to their own. If my people could see the deliverance of their ancestors centuries earlier by the hand of God, perhaps they could maintain their loyalty and faith long enough to outlast this evil man, Antiochus. Perhaps you will find that in what I wrote, there is also a message for you.

One of the distinctly Jewish practices was the observance of dietary regulations. We have what we call the kosher laws. We are not permitted to mix certain foods, such as meat and milk. And there are some foods, such as pork, which we are not allowed to eat at all. Knowing this, Antiochus devised a test requiring every Jew to eat pork. What would our people do, die or give in? Many of our people died rather than to defile themselves, but there were some people whose faith was wavering. How could I help them?

I told this story: Once, a long time ago, when our people were taken into exile by Nebuchadnezzar, king of Babylon, four of our finest young men were selected to be trained as pages for the king of Babylon. This meant that, unlike the rest of our people, they would live well and dine sump-tuously, eating food right from the king's table. But that would also mean foregoing the dietary restrictions which were part of their faith. Therefore, Daniel, one of the four young men, petitioned for them to have the right to eat only vegetables and to drink only water during their three years of training. Their trainer granted them a ten-day trial peri-od, during which time, if they became weaker, they would have to accept the king's bounty. After ten days, the young men were found to be stronger than all the rest who were in preparation, so they were able to continue their special diet. And not only that, but when they were finally presented to the king, he found these four young men to be superior in learning, wisdom, letters, and skills to all the advisers of the king, for God had honored their loyalty, and it brought about these good results. Therefore, Daniel, and the three others, Shadrack, Meshack, and Abednego became chief counselors to the king.

With such a story I sought to encourage my people to keep the dietary laws that made us Jewish. And is there not meaning here for your day as well? Are not many of you exiles from your accustomed home, required to live far from the place of your birth? Are not many of you living in strange surroundings among people with very different customs? And is it not a great temptation to throw off the traditions in which you were raised and to go against principles, because in your new setting you feel anonymous? I want to remind you that God is with you wherever you go, and you will not easily be shed of him. The only lasting happiness is to be found in a life that accords with what you already know to be God's will. That is what Daniel found.

On another occasion, Antiochus desecrated our temple in Jerusalem. In the courtyard of the temple was a place where we offered our sacrifices to God. Antiochus came into that place and set up an altar to Olympian Zeus, right on top of our own sacred altar, and he commanded that all Jews worship Zeus. We called this the "abomination that makes desolate." Immediately, the temple was emptied, and for three-and-one-half years no offering was made to God at that altar. There were some who felt that it would be better to give in to the tyrant than to die and leave Israel without any children. But what good are children to Israel, if they are not loyal to Israel's God?

To answer this I again told a story about Daniel's friends. Once upon a time, in the days of Daniel, King Nebuchadnezzar set up an image of gold, whose height was ninety feet and whose breadth was nine feet. He commanded all of his officials to come to the dedication. Daniel was not present, but Shadrack, Meshack, and Abednego were there. The heralds of the king commanded that at the right time, everyone present was to fall down and worship the image King Nebuchadnezzar had set up. Whoever did not, would be cast into the fiery furnace. When the time came, the three young men did not bow, and some of the other counselors of the king who were jealous of them, reported this to the king.

The king gave the three another chance, and when they still refused, because they were loyal to the Lord their God, the king became furious and ordered them to be thrown into the furnace, saying, "Who is the God that will deliver you out of my hand?" The three young men answered the king saying, "Our God, whom we serve, is able to deliver us from the fiery furnace, and he will deliver us out of your hand, O king. But if not, be it known to you, O king, that we will not serve your gods or worship the golden image which you have set up." Then the king had the young men thrown into the furnace. But after a time, the king saw the three young men walking around in the midst of the flame with another person whom the king himself described as "a son of the gods." The king called the young men out and finding them unharmed, he praised the God of Shadrack, Meshack, and Abednego, who had delivered them, and he made a decree that any nation, people, or language that spoke anything against the God of Shadrack, Meshack, and Abednego should be torn limb from limb and their houses laid in ruins, for, he said, there is no other God who is able to deliver in this way.

In such a manner I tried to keep alive the loyalty of my people to their God. But is there not something here for people of your age also? Do you not find it easier to adjust to evil than to stand up against it? Isn't it true of your time, as it was of mine, that people are always excusing themselves by saying of a questionable act, "Everybody is doing it"? Isn't it true that many people bow down to the false gods of your day, things like status, position, success, money, or security? Do they do it because there are so few who will refuse to do so? Isn't it true that what the world needs is more people of character who put their trust in God, regardless of the consequences? To live by faith means to live in disregard of the consequences, as those three young men did, even when God does not spare us the painful results of our loyalty.

On another occasion, Antiochus robbed the treasury of our temple. When he conquered our land, he assumed that all the offices were his to fill. The highest office we had was that of high priest. Antiochus sold that office to the highest bidder, and then, when that man was away somewhere, he sold the office to another man, Menelaus, for a higher price. Menelaus then plotted to steal and sell the temple vessels in order to recoup the cost of buying the office. When we Jews protested, Antiochus himself came and plundered the city and made off with the temple vessels. My people wondered if God could still be God and permit these things to happen. Where was justice?

It was at this point that I told another story about Daniel. Nebuchadnezzar had been dead for several years, and Belshazzar was reigning in his place. Belshazzar was having a great feast in the city of Babylon for a thousand of his lords. When everyone was filled with wine and merriment, Belshazzar happened to remember the golden vessels which Nebuchadnezzar had taken from the temple in Jerusalem years before. He thought, "What an interesting thing it would be to drink wine from a holy vessel." So he sent for the vessels and served wine in them to his lords, his wives, and his concubines. And as they drank, they praised the gods of gold, silver, bronze, iron, wood, and stone. Immediately, the fingers of a human hand appeared and wrote words on the wall of the king's palace. The king's color changed, and his thoughts alarmed him; his limbs gave way, and his knees knocked together. He called for someone to interpret the words that were written, and eventually, Daniel was called.

When Daniel entered the banquet hall, he saw the sacrilegious things the king had done; making merry with sacred vessels, praising gods which neither see, nor hear, nor know, and dishonoring the God who created him; and Daniel said as much to the king. The writing on the wall was "Mene, Mene, Tekel, and Parsin," and Daniel's interpretation of the matter was this: Mene: God has numbered in the days of your kingdom and brought it to an end. Tekel: you have been weighed in the balances and found wanting. Parsin: your kingdom is divided and given to the Medes and Persians. That very night, Belshazzar was slain, and his kingdom given to Darius the Mede.

With such a story, I attempted to console my people over the loss of our temple vessels. God was not powerless, and in time, Antiochus, too, would be brought to judgment.

I believe there's something here for you as well. In life there are always people who are drifting toward the time of judgment, as was Belshazzar in his day. Sometimes the drift is so gradual that they do not notice it. There is feasting and merrymaking right up to the last moment, without any sense that perhaps life was given to them for some better purpose. If they ever think about the time when they will give an accounting for their lives, they console themselves that it is still a long way off. Then, quite suddenly, they are at the brink. Had they only been alert, there would have been many opportunities to amend their ways. But now the end has come, and all that might have been is left behind.

A final impudence of Antiochus was his claim to be a god. He claimed to be Zeus reincarnated. He thought he looked like Zeus, and for that reason, he took on the title "Epiphanes," meaning "Divine Manifestation." Those of us under his rule had a different title for him: we called him "Epimanes," meaning "Madman." He did indeed eventually go mad and die while on a campaign in Persia, but not before he made many Jews choose between worshiping him or worshiping God.

To strengthen those who might be brought to the test, I told one more story about Daniel. Darius had become king now, in place of Belshazzar, and he had elevated Daniel to the second position in the land. Those who were under Daniel were jealous of his position and planned his disgrace. They persuaded the king that he should issue a decree that for a month no one should make any request of God or man except through the king, on pain of being thrown to the lions. This requirement was intended to show that the only way to God was through the king. Daniel knew of the decree, but he nevertheless prayed to God three times a day in the privacy of his room. His enemies were waiting for him, however, and accused him to the king. The king had no recourse but to have Daniel thrown into the den of lions, but the king already could see the error of his presumption, and as Daniel was led away, the king said to him, "May your God, whom you serve continually, deliver you." The king went to his palace, but could not sleep. The next morning, he went in haste to the lions' den, and found that Daniel was still alive, for the angel of God had shut the lions' mouths. So Daniel was pulled up out of the lions' den, and no kind of hurt was found upon him, because he had trusted his God.

Now, perhaps my stories about Daniel are a bit unsophisticated for people of your background. Perhaps you question whether those things ever happened the way I told them. Well, I'm not saying whether they were historical events or not, I'm just saying that they contain a lot of truths that the people in my day needed to hear.

And I suspect that the same need exists in your day. It isn't always a king's commands that keep people from worshiping God. Too often, I'm afraid, people find that they are just too busy for God. They tell themselves that there is just a certain amount of time for work, a certain amount for recreation, a certain amount with the family, and so their lives are lived without any religious disciplines whatsoever: no worship, no prayer, no study, no devotion. When the time of crisis comes, there is no inner resource that such people have developed, and they crumble under the strain. What is important is that in good times we develop a faith that can keep us in the bad times. My people remained loyal to God, and that loyalty kept them alive. Daniel remained loyal when the penalty was the lions' den, but it was the practice of his faith beforehand that gave him the courage to face his moment of truth. I do not know what you are called upon to face, but I am confident that the more you have practiced your faith before the time of trial, the more certain will be your victory. In your time of testing, I hope that you, too, will dare to be a Daniel.

The Bit Players Are Also Important: Joseph, Husband of Mary

Matthew 1:17-25

Prologue

In 1654, John Milton, poet and public servant, lost his sight. He felt placed on the sidelines after an active life. Seeking to declare that his was not over, he penned the lines: "They also serve, who only stand and wait." It was after he saw himself on the sidelines that he published one of the finest poetical works in the English language, *Paradise Lost*. Indeed, how often it is that one on the sidelines of a great event contributes much that is essential.

I have often thought of Joseph, the husband of Mary, as the man on the sidelines. I was once asked to play the part of Joseph in a Nativity play. I was honored. When I asked for the script, I was told that I wouldn't need a script. Joseph doesn't say anything; he just stands there leaning on a staff. I was crestfallen. Good, kind, understanding, helpful, Joseph I would be, but not a line would I speak. Joseph was a sideline character, essential, but not central. To say that Joseph was a sideline character does not mean that he was unimportant. I would like us to see the birth of Jesus through his eyes. I think we shall not only capture the mystery of Jesus' birth, but something of Joseph's importance to it, and, indeed, the importance of every person who endeavors to do God's will. Let Joseph speak for himself.

Would you believe a man who sees things — I mean, one who has visions? Pardon me, my name is Joseph. My family came originally from Bethlehem in Judea, but I have spent much of my life in a small town in Galilee, called Nazareth. That is why people call me Joseph of Nazareth. That question about visions was serious. Please, don't smile when I ask. I've seen visions, and they have altered the course of my life. In fact, I've seen some things even stranger than visions, and I've had a part in something great.

But that gets ahead of my story. Let me tell you something about myself. I am a fourteenth generation, of a fourteenth generation, of a fourteenth generation, which means that, according to our method of calculation, I can trace my heritage back fourteen generations to the Babylonian captivity, back another fourteen generations to King David, back still another fourteen generations to Abraham, the father of our people. That means I have the blood of King David himself in my veins. I could be a king. My son could be a king. But that isn't very likely this far removed from the source. And in a dominated country, who cares about your pedigree?

I am a carpenter by trade. I was living a contented life in Nazareth some years ago. I had a small shop, and I was engaged to be married. Our wedding date was growing near, when suddenly my life changed. Mary, my fiancée, came to me and told me she was going to have a baby. I got sick. I didn't know what to do. She insisted that this was an act of God. I couldn't believe that. I thought about it for several days. As I saw it, there were two choices: public trial or private divorce. Engagement is a very serious relationship in our culture. It can be broken only by divorce. I loved Mary, so I decided not to expose her to public ridicule but to break the engagement quietly.

That very night an angel appeared to me, corroborating Mary's story. He said, "Don't be afraid to take Mary for your wife. Her conception is from God." He said she would have a son, and his name would be called Jesus, a name that means "Jehovah is salvation." I was told that he would save his people from their sins. Up to that time in my life, I had not been a person given to visions, though it is interesting that my namesake in the days of early Israel was called "Joseph the dreamer." However, I am not like him; he was the favorite son of a great and wealthy sheik; I am but a village carpenter. Even so, I was convinced that God was calling me. So I took Mary as my wife.

In those days Augustus Caesar wanted all the people in the Roman empire to be counted for taxation purposes. He required that every person should go to his or her hometown to be counted in the census. I put off going as long as I could, because of Mary's condition. We hoped that we would be able to wait until the child was born. Bethlehem, my ancestral home, was ninety miles away, a journey of several days over rough roads. The deadline for enrollment was fast approaching, however, and still the child had not come. I could see that I, at least, had to go, but Mary refused to be left alone. The townspeople were talking. I took her along, hoping to make it to Bethlehem before the birth.

Bethlehem was terribly crowded. There was not a room to be had. The trip had brought Mary to her time. All I could find was a stall where animals were kept. There Mary had her child. His first bed was a feeding trough for animals! I began to doubt the message of my vision. If God had any interest in this birth, surely he could have done better than this! At least a room could have been provided! Perhaps there had been no vision. Perhaps I just wanted to convince myself out of love for Mary. How helpless I felt! How useless I was! How could I have allowed myself to get involved in all of this? I was angry with Mary for what I felt was a lie, angry with myself for being a party to this, and angry with God for letting me believe that I had had a vision of something great.

Then things began to change: shepherds came who claimed that they had heard a heavenly announcement; Eastern astrologers came from afar, claiming that they had seen a star; they brought gifts for the child and said that even King Herod over in Jerusalem was interested in this birth. I was dumbfounded to realize how much God's hand could be seen in all of this. It appeared as if God had prepared the whole universe for this moment! And he had also prepared me. I was not to be the central character, but I did have a role to play. After all, who had protected Mary thus far? Who had secured even this humble place? And who would care for mother and child now? All of these responsibilities, God had entrusted to me. Obviously, I would need his guidance more than ever. Perhaps my vision had been correct and had been given to prepare me for my task.

After some days, we decided to go to Jerusalem. You see, there is a custom among our people that a firstborn son belongs to God. That goes all the way back to the Passover in Egypt, when the firstborn were redeemed by a sacrifice. Therefore, Jewish parents make a sacrifice in the temple, in effect, to buy back their first son from God. Besides, forty days after a birth, a woman is supposed to purify herself in the temple. Since Jerusalem was only five miles from Bethlehem, we thought we would go there for a while.

In fact, we considered staying in Jerusalem permanently. The gifts would help us to rent a place, and I could open a shop. We weren't sure how we would be received back in Nazareth. The day came when we made our offering in the temple. That same day, and aged man named Simeon made a great fuss over Jesus. He said that he had been promised that he would not die until he had seen Israel's Messiah. He picked up Jesus in his arms and cried for joy, saying that he could now die in peace, for he had seen the Messiah. But, he said that Jesus would be spoken against, and Mary would suffer sorrow. An aged prophetess, Anna, also saw Jesus and gave thanks to God.

I thought our worries were over. If this child was to grow up to be the Messiah, Israel's deliverer, as these aged visionaries had said, what could go wrong? Yet, that very night God spoke to me again in a dream: "Go to Egypt, for Herod is going to seek the child to kill him." We left that very night,

I on foot, and Mary and the child on a donkey, and made our way to Egypt, even as my namesake, the other Joseph, had done so many centuries before. We stayed in Egypt for two years. I took odd jobs to sustain us, and the gifts of those strange men from the East helped us to survive.

Eventually, the time came for us to return to Palestine. We had heard the news that Herod had died. I received another vision from God that convinced me it was safe to return. I couldn't help thinking, as we left Egypt, of those words of the prophet Hosea, where God speaks of Israel and says, "Out of Egypt have I called my son." God was calling us out of Egypt, too. It was as though we were retracing the steps of our ancestors when they came across the desert to settle in the promised land. We thought we would go and settle in Jerusalem, for by now there would be nothing left in Nazareth anyway. But when I heard that Archelaus, Herod's son, was now ruling in the place of his father, I felt that it would be safer to return to the small village of Nazareth, than to chance an encounter in Jerusalem, for Archelaus was no better than his father.

I opened a carpentry shop in Nazareth, and all the years he was growing up, Jesus worked with me and learned my trade. But all the while I was training him, I knew that he had a destiny beyond my comprehension, and it wouldn't involve carpentry. When he was about thirty years old, he came to me and said that he was going to leave Nazareth. He felt a call to teach, and he had to answer it. I understood. I had been expecting it for some time. I was grateful that he had stayed with us as long as he had. We have heard some great things about him in these months that he's been away. I'm only sorry that I'm too old and too stiff to follow him around and hear some of the things he has to say. Sometimes he comes back to Nazareth, and we catch up on how things are going with him. Some people hang on his every word; others are quite critical and wonder out loud where he gets his authority for the things he says. Their anger worries us. We wish he wouldn't be so outspoken. But there's nothing we can do about that, so we have simply put him in God's hands. God, no doubt, has something more for him to do.

What never ceases to amaze me is how God consented to use me in his plans. No, more than that, God made me *essential* to his plans, even though I know I have not been the central character. I'm just a simple man, as you've heard from my story; not much when compared with kings and statesmen. Yet, I have learned the truth of that saying: "They also serve, who only stand and wait." God honored my service. He made me his partner in the advancement of Jesus' ministry and that has given my life meaning.

That brings me around to the point I wanted to make through my story, and it is simply this: regardless of who you are, no matter how insignificant you think your position is, God has a place for you. When you live your life in humble service to any of God's children, God accepts that as service to himself and that makes every one of us important.

The House of Bread: Balthazar

Matthew 2:1-12

It was in the year 3758 according to the Jewish scriptures when Melchior and Caspar and I made our great journey. It was a long time ago, when I was younger. It was in the year 752 from the founding of the city of Rome, if you figure it that way. Herod was king of the Jews, and the whole world was at peace.

My name is Balthazar. My friends Caspar and Melchoir and I were astrologers, discerners of the meaning of heavenly signs. It was our business to study the stars and ancient writings in order that we might advise the Persian rulers on matters of politics. For centuries, we Persians have had living among us people of Jewish extraction who have perpetuated their history and legends, and shared with us their sacred writings. One of their legends is that at the birth of two of their great patriarchs, Isaac and Moses, new stars appeared in the heavens. Naturally, this made us astrologers interested in these people. They even produced certain writings from their history that spoke of some such occurrence yet to be. In the book of Numbers, it says, "A star shall come forth out of Jacob, and a scepter shall arise out of Israel" (Numbers 24:17). It was in the nature of our business to keep that in mind, for we astrologers have long believed that a star could be an angel or a heavenly counterpart of a great man. The Jews among us said such a star would appear when their messiah was born.

About the time I have mentioned, in year 52 of Octavian Augustus, a strange thing took place. The planets, Jupiter and Saturn, came into close conjunction three times in one year, giving the appearance of one bright star. "Surely," we thought, "this is the star of the Jews." We took it as an omen and determined that such a person, whose birth was announced by the heavens, must surely be worth seeing. Therefore, with the permission of our king, we set off for Israel, expecting to honor a new king. My life has not been the same since, and I would like to share with you some of my observations.

One thing that sticks in my mind is the whole situation at Jerusalem. It was understandable that we should head for Jerusalem. After all, kings are generally born in palaces and one would expect a royal birth to take place there. At the same time, we were aware of certain problems in our reckoning, for Herod was king in Jerusalem. Herod had on different occasions murdered his wife and three of his sons. Herod had married ten different women. Herod, whose treachery and jealousy were known everywhere. Herod, who, though king of the Jews, was not himself a Jew, could he be the father of "a star out of Jacob"?

Nonetheless, we had no choice but to head for Jerusalem. Yet, upon our arrival in Jerusalem we could detect no rejoicing, no celebrating of a king's birth such as the presence of a heavenly sign might lead us to expect. We Gentiles had traveled hundreds of miles to do homage to a Jewish king, but the Jews did not even seem to be aware of his birth. It was this absence of festivity that made us cautious. It wouldn't do to march right up to the palace uninvited and ask to see the new heir. Perhaps Herod was keeping it a secret. Or perhaps our expectation was all wrong. Herod being the kind of man he was, who knows what he might have done? So we began asking townspeople, "Where is the one who has been born king of the Jews?" The people were ignorant of any such happening, but one of them apparently took our questioning to the palace, for it was not long before we were requested to appear at a royal audience.

We went before Herod and told him our story. He said there was no new child in his palace. We were willing to admit that the error was ours, and to return home, but Herod was troubled and asked us to stay. That same evening, unknown to us, he called together his religious leaders and students of the sacred writings and asked them where the messiah should be born when the time came. His counselors referred to one of their ancient prophets, Micah, a writing we did not have, for the answer. Micah had said years before, "And you, O Bethlehem, are by no means least among the rulers of Judah, for from you shall come a ruler who shall govern my people, Israel" (Micah 5:2).

Armed with this information, Herod called us back again secretly to tell us that the one we sought might be in Bethlehem, a small town about five miles to the south. In fact, he spoke as though he fully expected we would be successful in our search. He asked us to be sure to stop back and tell him where the child was so that he could go and honor him, too. We thanked him for his help, but made no answer.

No sooner had we started again on our journey than the star appeared once more. This time it seemed to hang in the sky almost directly above us. It appeared as though shafts of light were pointing directly down to the little town in the distance, Bethlehem. What a strange name that is for a town, "Bethlehem." It means "House of Bread." As we passed by wheat fields white in the moonlight, it occurred to me that perhaps that was not such a strange name after all, for this town obviously met the hunger for bread for a large number of people. And what would we find at the House of Bread? Something to satisfy our hunger, too? Our hunger was not for bread, but for something that our worship of the elements — earth, air, fire, and water, had never given us — a personal experience with the living God.

A humble shepherd boy showed us the only place where, as far as he knew, there was a newborn baby. It was a rather simple house, hardly the place one would look for a king or anyone whose birth was heralded by a star. But the star did seem to be sending rays down upon that house. We dismounted and went to the door. A man came to the door who said his name was Joseph. He was astonished at our presence but received us cordially. He told us of shepherds who had come previously to the manger where the child was born, speaking of an angel that had guided them. Such tidings convinced us that we had found the right place, and we asked if we, too, might see the child.

When we saw him, it was not like anything we had expected! What a contrast with Jerusalem! There we had seen Herod in regal splendor and here we saw a child in poverty. There Herod had been surrounded by retainers and dignitaries, here this child and his parents were unbefriended. In Jerusalem, Herod reigned with absolute power; here, a helpless child lay. There a crafty politician, here an infant in all its innocence. Yet, there was a majesty about the child that caused us to bow in reverence.

We honored him there and offered the gifts we had brought. Caspar offered gold, a gift to crown a king; for if the star was right, a king he would be. Melchoir offered frankincense, the essence of prayer to God. I brought myrrh, the bitter spice of sorrow, for a person such as he, born in such humble surroundings, was bound to know sorrow, if he should ever try to fulfill the destiny suggested by the star.

We left that place with a great sense of peace. We had come to the House of Bread and our hunger had been satisfied. We looked up into the sky and found that the star was gone. But then, it had served its purpose. It had declared God's great pleasure at this birth, and it had brought us Gentiles to see what God was about to do. This child was himself the Star of Jacob, the Deliverer, not only of Israel, but of all people. And as we had been drawn from the east to pay homage to him, we felt that one day others would be drawn from east, west, north, and south to honor him and that through him, they would find God.

The star has disappeared from the sky, but the Star of Jacob is shining yet, and those who follow him will find, as we did, that they have been brought close to God.

In an Upper Room:
John Mark

Mark 14:12-26

All week, Jewish pilgrims had been arriving in Jerusalem. They were coming for the annual Passover Festival, the great central event in our lives as a people. I was a resident in Jerusalem at the time — just a young man — under twenty years of age. My name is John Mark. In subsequent years, I traveled with Peter and Paul. But at the time about which I have been telling you, I lived with my parents, who had become secret followers of Jesus of Nazareth.

At the beginning of that particular week, Jesus had come into Jerusalem riding on a donkey. He had received a rather noisy reception by some of the people, who felt that he was announcing his intention to become a leader. The next day he went to the temple where he overturned the tables of the men who had the profitable money-changing concession there. He interfered with those who sold sacrificial animals to the pilgrims. During the next several days, he challenged the authority of the temple officers, brought into question the traditions of our Jewish religion, and made himself unpopular with those who had vested interests in the status quo. We learned later that the authorities sought to arrest him, but they didn't want to do it publicly for fear of arousing the people. They let their interest be known, however, and unknown to any of us, Judas, one of Jesus' own disciples, made arrangements to assist in Jesus' arrest. For these reasons it was becoming more and more dangerous for Jesus to go about openly in the city.

Nevertheless, he had come to Jerusalem with his disciples for the purpose of celebrating the Passover. Thursday was drawing near, the evening of which was the time when the Passover meal would be eaten. My parents knew that Jesus did not have a place to share that meal with his friends, so they quietly made mention of the fact that he could use our upper room if he chose. Most of the houses in Jerusalem are single-room buildings, like simple square boxes. Some of them have an upper room, like a small box on top of a larger one that is reached by an outside staircase. It was such a room that my parents were offering.

In the light of the growing official hostility to Jesus, my parents felt it would be wiser not to be too open about their contacts with Jesus, so they made an arrangement with him. Jesus was to send two of his disciples, who were to prepare the meal, to a fountain in our section of the city, where they would see a man with a water jar. He would be easy enough to recognize, because in our country, it is generally women who carry the water. The disciples were to follow the man to our house where they would meet my father, who would then show them the room. I was the one who carried the water pot. All of this took place as I have said, and the upper room was made ready.

That evening, Jesus came into the city with his disciples, and they walked as inconspicuously as possible to our house where they climbed the outside stairs, two or three men at a time, in order to avoid attention. I stood in the shadows of the room, ready to help in any way I could, should Jesus or his friends need my service. Flickering oil lamps lighted the room. A few words of blessing were spoken, and the meal was begun. There seemed to be little joy in this gathering. The disciples were tense, fidgety, and uneasy. Before they had come to Jerusalem on this trip, Jesus had told them that he was going to his death. They hadn't believed him or hadn't understood him, but now they were beginning to see the possibility of his death looming before them. Not only were they worried about him, but as his close associates, they were worried about their own safety as well.

The first thing that comes to my mind as I recall that scene is an action on the part of Jesus. Apparently there had been a breakdown of friendly relations within the group. The disciples had been talking — I suppose one could say quarreling — about precedence and status within the group, and the sultry weather only aggravated their irritability. Fear, anger, and jealousy were simmering in the hearts of those men.

The meal was begun in silence. Then, unexpectedly, and without uttering a word, Jesus arose and poured water from a jug into a large basin. He tied a large towel around his waist, and proceeded to wash the dusty feet of each of his friends and to wipe them with the towel. Ordinarily, a host would have a servant available to wash the feet of his guests, but on that night, the Master, playing the role of a servant, did this for his friends. Simon Peter offered some resistance, but Jesus assured him that this was the way it had to be. When Jesus had finished, he said, "If I, your Lord and Teacher, have washed your feet, you also ought to wash one another's feet. For I have given you an example, that you should do as I have done." Wow! Did that ever change things! This incident, this acted out parable, set the disciples straight about precedence and status. No longer was each concerned about whether he was getting the prominence he deserved; every one of them was called to be a servant!

The second thing I remember about that evening is how Jesus startled the group by declaring that one of them was about to betray him. Each of them protested that that was impossible. "Is it I?" they would say, "Is it I?" Each one felt that his relationship was secure enough that such a thing could not happen. All of us in that room were to learn differently. Each of us would discover just how human we were.

I am sure you know that it was Judas who betrayed him. Jesus said to him, "What you are going to do, do quickly." Judas left the room, but the others gave no thought to his exit. They assumed that Jesus was simply telling him to go out and buy something, because he was the one who carried the purse for the group.

Though the betrayal by Judas was premeditated, each of us, later that evening, participated in a denial of our relationship to Jesus. When the meal was over, the disciples went out to the Mount of Olives on their way back to Bethany, the town where they were staying. I accompanied them, carrying a lantern for their benefit. When the soldiers came to arrest Jesus, each of the disciples fled, and so did I. A soldier grabbed hold of my robe, and I ran off naked into the night, leaving my robe in his hands. Perhaps that is the reason why I remember so well those words about betrayal. Jesus knew how weak we were, but he loved us anyway. In subsequent years, I have failed again and again to stand up for Jesus, but I am confident that, in spite of my weaknesses, he loves me still.

But let me talk more about the upper room. The third thing I remember about that night is the breaking of the bread. When the meal was completed, Jesus quietly took a piece of bread and offered a brief prayer over it. Then he broke it, and gave it to his disciples saying, "This is my body, which is given for you. Do this in remembrance of me." The disciples each took a part of it, not really knowing what it meant. Then he took a cup, and when he offered thanks over it, he gave that to his disciples saying, "This cup which is poured out for you is the new covenant in my blood." They all drank from it solemnly, still not quite knowing what to make of it.

"Do this in remembrance of me," he said. Not only did those disciples partake of those simple elements that night, but thereafter, whenever they, or any of us who were followers of Jesus, gathered, we broke bread together and thought about Jesus. It started as such a simple act. Over the years it became more and more formalized. But always the intention was the same: to remember Jesus. It is not a mere memorial of someone who died. It is a commemoration of his death, of his resurrection, and of his presence with us even now. For me, the bread and the wine have become symbolic of Jesus' spirit. As any food becomes fuel, to give our bodies energy so that we can function, so those elements remind us that the spirit of Jesus dwells in each of us, giving us spiritual direction and energy so that we can function for Christ. He dwells in your body and in my body, and when we stoop to serve, as he stooped to serve, then we become the Body of Christ, doing his work in the world.

The Man Who Was Born Blind: Nathan

John 9:1-8

Have you ever had a stroke of good fortune, and then discovered that no one was able to rejoice with you? I have had such an experience — it changed my life — and it opened my eyes — in more ways than one. My name is Nathan. I was a resident of Jerusalem in the days of Jesus. I was born blind, and I used to sit at the temple gate asking for alms from those who went in and out. Some things that Jesus did and said had a tremendous impact on my life, and I'd like to share them with you, for I feel that they can add something to your life as well.

The first thing I should do is to tell you exactly what happened. I was seated near the temple one sabbath day begging alms, as I have said. I was hoping for a few coins just to keep going from day-to-day. Little did I realize the gift that I was about to receive, and the stir that it would make. Being sightless, my hearing was quite acute. I heard a group of men passing by, and I heard one of them say, obviously in reference to me; "Teacher, whose sin was it that caused that man to be born blind? Was it his own or his parent's sin?" That was no new question for me. I had heard that question debated before. It seemed obvious to everyone that my blindness must be the result of somebody's sin. Not only did I have to suffer sightlessness, I had to bear the opprobrium that this was somehow punishment. No one had answered the questions satisfactorily, but everyone agreed that the blindness had been sent by God.

I waited for the one they called "Teacher" to give his opinion of where the sin lay. But the teacher, whom I later learned to be Jesus, gave a completely different answer. "His blindness has nothing to do with his sins or his parent's sins. Rather, God's power is going to be seen at work in him." What a liberating thought that was! I might be blind, but he was saying that it was not a punishment as a result of sin. Praise God for such a teacher! Then I heard him spit on the ground, and mix the spittle with some dirt to make mud. The next thing I knew, he was rubbing the mud on my closed eyes. I didn't know what was going on, but I was frightened, and I couldn't get away. Then he said in a quiet and assuring voice, "Go wash your face in the pool of Siloam." His voice quieted my fears, and I made my way to the pool that was not far away.

When I washed my face, I was suddenly able to see! Oh, the colors! The brilliance! The faces! The people! The sky! I saw a donkey for the first time! I saw a building! I grabbed shopkeepers whom I had known for years and looked into their faces. When they asked how this had happened, I could only say that the man named Jesus had done it. When they asked, "Where is he?" I had to confess that I didn't know.

Naturally, word of this got to our spiritual leaders, and I was taken to them. I thought they would rejoice with me at the great blessing which had come into my life. Instead, they asked solemnly what had happened. I told them about Jesus, and about the mud, and about washing in the pool. Do you know what some of them said? They said, "Obviously, the man who did this cannot be from God, because he doesn't obey the sabbath laws against working on the sabbath!" I couldn't believe it! A great thing like this had happened in their midst, and they were saying that it shouldn't have happened because it was the sabbath! Then they said to me, "You say he opened your eyes. Well, what do you say about him?" I said, "He must be a prophet!" They didn't like that answer, and they began to disbelieve that I had ever been blind in the first place. They sent for my parents and asked if I was their son. Then they asked if I had in fact been born blind, and if so, how did they explain the fact that I could now see? My parents affirmed that I was their son, and that I had been born blind, but they were plainly nervous about my being able to see now. There were no congratulations, no praising God for a miracle; only evidence of fear. I later learned that the spiritual leaders had already agreed that if anyone professed that Jesus was the Messiah, he would be excommunicated. That was why my parents were fearful and unable to rejoice at my good fortune.

The leaders then wanted me to agree that Jesus was a sinner. I told them, "I don't know if he is a sinner or not. I only know that I was blind, and now I can see!" When they wanted to hear the story again, I asked if they wanted to hear it so that they, too, might become disciples of Jesus. They became angry and cursed me and said that they were disciples of Moses, who they were sure spoke for God, but this Jesus, they said, they did not know about. By now, I was incensed at their hardness of heart, and I said, "This is strange. You are spiritual leaders, he has opened my eyes, and you say you don't know where he comes from. Unless this man came from God, he wouldn't be able to do a thing like this." They couldn't accept my assessment, and they excommunicated me — kicked me out of the synagogue and took away my religious affiliation.

A little later, Jesus found me. I knew right away from his voice that it was he. He asked if I believed in him, and I answered, "I believe, Lord." Just a few hours before that I had not known that he existed; then he came to me as a man out of nowhere; then I had confessed him to be a prophet; now, I've bowed before him, and called him "Lord." It was strange, too, that I, who had been born blind, could see so clearly who Jesus was, while those spiritual leaders, who should have been able to see the truth in Jesus, were blinded by their unbelief. Thus far, I had experienced a marvelous physical experience, but Jesus was about to build on that and turn it into a spiritual lesson for me and for others.

That brings me to the second thing I want to do, which is to share with you some of Jesus' teachings related to this incident. Some of the spiritual leaders, who were his enemies, and some other people, had gathered around me to see what Jesus would say. He addressed his remarks to me, but it was obvious that he intended other people to hear what he had to say. He referred to the characteristics of the good shepherd. He pointed out how a good shepherd stays by his flock when danger is near. He doesn't desert the flock, but rises to their defense, even laying down his own life if necessary. The spiritual leaders of my religion had been far more interested in protecting themselves and their status than to ministering to me as one of their flock. Jesus spoke of the relationship of caring that exists between the good shepherd and his sheep. He reminded those of us who were listening of the manner in which a shepherd can call his sheep by name, and how his sheep know his voice and come to him because he's taken an interest in them individually. The spiritual leaders of my religion had not cared about me as an individual. In fact, when I had cause to rejoice, they saw me only as a nuisance. Jesus spoke of the shepherd leading his sheep from the fold — going before them to show them the way. I, on the other hand, had been thrust out of the fold — cut off from the flock — with nowhere to go.

By means of such an allegory, Jesus was, of course, speaking to my condition, and to that of a good many people who felt alone and uncared for. When he announced that he had come to be that good shepherd, I was ready to become part of his flock. I have learned over the years since then that he is indeed a good shepherd. I believe he laid down his life out of his love for his flock. His interest in individuals assures me that the God whom he called Father is interested in us as individuals. He has shown me that I cannot really be cut off from God by the actions of other people. No matter what people may do to me, I am a part of God's flock — no one can take that relationship away from me.

The other image Jesus used was that of the door to a sheepfold. To understand that, you need to visualize what a sheepfold in my part of the world looks like. It is simply an open space out on a hillside that is enclosed by rock walls. It has an opening, but no gate. At night, the shepherd takes his flock into the enclosure for protection from wolves and thieves. Then the shepherd himself lies in the opening to act as a door. No one can enter to harm the sheep without the shepherd rising to their protection, and no sheep can wander out and become lost without the knowledge of the shepherd.

Jesus stated that he was such a door and I have found him to be so. Through him, I have come into intimate contact with God. Through him, I have come to experience the fullness of life that he said he came to bring. Through him I have come into contact with the flock of God's people. He is, indeed, a door to life.

I have told you all this, not to entertain you, but to testify to the importance of Jesus Christ in my life. Perhaps you, too, need someone to open your eyes so that you can see what is important. Perhaps you, too, need a shepherd to guide your steps. Perhaps you, too, need a door through which you can enter fully to life. Jesus provided those things for me. If you let him, I'm sure he will do the same for you.

An Emmaus Disciple:
Cleopas

Luke 24:13-35

As I think back on it now, the day was probably bright and sunny on that spring Sunday so long ago, but none of us were really in the mood to notice it. Birds may have been singing but we did not notice them either. My wife, Hephsebah, and I were making our way back from Jerusalem to our home in Emmaus, about seven miles away. Many disturbing things had happened during the preceding week, and now, as we walked and talked, we were trying to sort them out.

Let me introduce myself. My name is Cleopas. My wife, Hephsebah, and I had both been followers of Jesus of Nazareth ever since he had visited our village a couple of years earlier. We had listened to his words, we had seen his mighty deeds, and we had figured that surely he was the one we Jews had long been waiting for, the one who was going to redeem Israel. We were among those who had cheered him on when, on the previous Sunday, he had entered Jerusalem, accompanied by great acclamation. When things went badly and he was arrested, we were among those waiting by Pilate's palace on Friday for some word of his fate. We were also among those who looked on in utter disbelief as the finest man who ever lived was nailed to a cross and killed. When it was over, we stayed with his close associates, the eleven, on Friday night. We stayed Saturday night too, because of the restriction against walking any great distance on the sabbath.

But now that the sabbath was over, there wasn't much reason to stay around Jerusalem. We were all holed up in a secret room on a back street in Jerusalem with the doors bolted and the windows covered, waiting for a fateful knock at the door that would indicate that the authorities had come for us, too. We talked in low whispers about our executed leader, wondering how we could avoid the same fate. It was no spiritual feast, I can tell you, for each of us was afraid even to trust the other. After all, it had been one of Jesus' closest disciples who had betrayed him to the authorities. Who could we trust? All of us were disillusioned, demoralized, and afraid; afraid to stay together, afraid to separate.

While we debated what to do, Mary Magdalene and a couple of the other women who had been close to Jesus, came rushing into the place where most of us were staying, crying and shouting that Jesus' body was missing. They had gone to the tomb to prepare Jesus' body more properly for burial, because they hadn't been able to do it on Friday evening. On Saturday, the sabbath restrictions prohibited them from working, so they had set out early Sunday morning to do it. They were now screaming excitedly about the tomb being open, about a heavenly messenger, and about the body being gone. We thought they were overwrought, but to satisfy them, Peter and John went to have a look. They, too, came back declaring that the tomb was empty. The body of Jesus was nowhere to be found. Hephsebah and I figured this was some kind of action taken by the temple authorities to keep Jesus' tomb from becoming a shrine for his followers. If we were correct, it would mean that the authorities hadn't forgotten about Jesus' followers either, and it would be best to get out of Jerusalem as quickly as possible.

Taking our leave of the eleven and the others, we set out toward the west, toward the setting sun, which matched our spirits, for as far as we were concerned the sun had indeed set for Israel. With leaden feet and sagging hopes we made our way along the road to Emmaus, retelling and talking over the events, attempting to make the pain go away. It was along that road that we had a strange experience that I would like to share with you.

It was about dusk when a man came up and asked to join us along the road. That was not strange, for robbers could be anywhere on such a road, and it was always better for travelers to form groups. Hephsebah and I continued our conversation. The man listened for a while and then asked, "What is all this that you are talking about?" I stopped and looked at him and said, "Are you the only person living in Jerusalem who doesn't know what has been happening there these past few days?" "What things?" he asked. "Why, the things that happened to Jesus of Nazareth," I said. Then I proceeded to tell him about Jesus' life and teachings, about our crushed hopes, the missing body, and about how wrong we must have been.

When he heard what I had to say, this man who had just joined us began to take us to task for giving up on Jesus. I didn't see how we could do anything but give up, but this fellow proceeded to say, "Don't you know that this is what the scriptures have said all along was going to happen to the Christ?" Then, for the next few miles, as we walked, he went through the various books of our Bible, showing us passage after passage in which it was prophesied that the Messiah would experience the very things Jesus had gone through. It was uncanny how he knew so much about the life of Jesus, but we were so interested in what he was saying that we gave little thought to that.

Let me share with you some of the things he pointed out: He recalled to us the words to Abraham, that one day Abraham's people would bring a blessing to all the families of earth. He reminded us that, as Moses had lifted up a serpent on a stick to save his people from death in the wilderness, even so must someone be lifted up on a stick to help people focus their faith in God. He called to mind the promise which Moses had made that another prophet like himself would one day arise to lead his people. He referred to Isaiah's words about the coming of Emmanuel, "God with us," and about the one to be called "Wonderful Counselor, Everlasting Father, Prince of Peace." He spent considerable time on those words of Isaiah about the servant who must suffer for his people, you know, "the man of sorrow, acquainted with grief." He went on to remind us of Daniel's words about the "Son of Man," a title Jesus often used of himself. Then from Micah he lifted up the prophecy about one to be born in Bethlehem, where Jesus had been born. He even lifted up those words from Zechariah about someone coming into Zion riding on a donkey, as Jesus had done only a week before. He referred to those words from Psalm 22, "My God, my God, why hast thou forsaken me?" which Jesus had also uttered from the cross. And then, finally, he mentioned those cryptic words from Psalm 16 about God not allowing his holy one to remain in the grave.

That last part we didn't understand at the time, but we were awestruck at this man's command of the scripture and at his ability to relate it to Jesus. These were passages that we had known, but we had never thought to apply them to Jesus. It was as though a veil had been lifted from our eyes so that we could see Jesus in places we had never thought to look. We were being taught to see that Christ comes to life in the Bible.

We were soon to discover that Christ comes alive in other ways. By now we had arrived at our village. It appeared that our companion intended to go on, but the light was fast fading, so we invited him to come into our house and stay with us. He consented and came in.

Hephsebah prepared a simple meal and we sat down together in dim candlelight to share food around the table. We asked him to offer the blessing. Then a strange thing happened. He took the loaf of bread, blessed it, broke it, and offered it to us. It was then that we saw the wounds in his hands. Our eyes were suddenly opened! How could we have been so blind? Our guest was Jesus himself! We knew him when he broke the bread. Death had not held him. We can't explain how that could be; we can only testify that Jesus was alive and we knew it.

We've thought about that incident a lot since it happened. It occurs to me that what Jesus was attempting to point out is that he comes among us in the simplest of things: table fellowship, the sharing of food, the blessing of bread and wine. When we who follow him share these things, in some mystical way he comes among us. Then, as soon as we became convinced that Jesus was really with us, he vanished. But we have discovered numerous times since then in the breaking of bread that he is still with us.

We were to discover him in still others ways. As soon as we collected our senses, Hephsebah and I decided to return at once to Jerusalem, to tell the eleven what we had experienced. When we arrived, we found the disciples and others of Jesus' followers still together in the upper room where they had been staying. But before we could even get our mouths open, they surrounded us and cried, "The Lord really has risen, and he has appeared to Peter." What a meeting that must have been! Peter, you can imagine, had felt dejected ever since the night of the trial, for he had denied even knowing Jesus, just as Jesus had said he would. But now Peter was radiant; things had been set straight between Peter and Jesus, and I guess Peter really knew what it meant to be forgiven.

We then told them what had happened to us on the road, and how Jesus had become known to us in the breaking of the bread. No sooner had we spoken, than Jesus himself appeared in our midst! The disciples were joyful, but frightened; relieved, but disbelieving. They felt they were seeing a ghost. Jesus sensed that and urged us to touch him. "I am not a ghost," he said, "It is really I." What I want to get across to you is that he made himself known to us in our fellowship. For the most part, he revealed himself to us when we were together. It was then that we remembered his words, "Where two or three are gathered in my name, there am I in the midst of them."

It has been a long time since that glorious Sunday when we became convinced that Jesus was alive. In the interval, we have asked ourselves often whether it really happened as I have said. Is it possible that we suffered an hallucination? Was it Jesus, or was it just wishful thinking, as others have suggested? I've thought about it quite a bit, and I'm still convinced that it really was Jesus.

Think what his resurrection means! It means that it is God who is finally in control; not Herod or Pilate, or those like them. It means that God is active in his world and cannot be defeated, even by death. It means that, though death is a real experience, it does not have the last word. It means that human personality endures and that character is more lasting than all those physical accumulations on which we focus our attention.

Now, why have I told you all this? You may think that it is to get you to believe that someone rose from the dead so many years ago. But if you come to such a belief on my account, it would simply mean that I am a convincing story-teller or that you consider me to be trustworthy. It still might not make any difference to you. What I have done is to witness to my experiences with the risen Lord. What I hope is that I have, at least, caught your interest so that you will ask, "What was so special about Jesus that some people became convinced that he rose from the dead?"

The question, then, is not one of passing historical interest, but one of pressing personal significance, for on its answer rests the whole matter of personal lifestyle. It is still possible to discover the living Lord in the circumstances which I have described: in the pages of scripture, which testify to him; in the mystery of breaking bread, as when we gather to remember him in communion; and in the fellowship of believers who gather in his name. If you will open your life and invite him in, as we invited him into our home in Emmaus, you will discover that *this* is Emmaus, that *every* day is the third day, and that he comes to live in you.

Peter on Pentecost:
Simon Peter

Acts 2:1-8

"Simon Barjona, fisherman." That was about the extent
of the notoriety I had experienced or ever wanted. I was a
simple villager from Galilee in northern Palestine. I had expected to live out my days there in business with my brother, Andrew. It was my brother who introduced me to Jesus,
a carpenter from Nazareth, who had become an itinerant
preacher. There was something so appealing about what
Jesus taught, and about how he lived, that when he asked
the two of us to travel around Palestine with him, we agreed.
During the course of the several years we spent with him,
I became convinced that Jesus was more than a teacher, so
when he asked me one day who I thought he was, I said,
"You are the Christ," the long-awaited Messiah. In response
he said, "And you are Peter, and on this rock I will build my
church." That last part was a play on words. My nickname
is Peter, or, "The Rock," because of my size and strength.
And Jesus was saying he was going to build his church on
me. Well, I guess I was flattered, but I really didn't know at
the time what a church was. The word he used was a Greek
word, meaning "a called out assembly," but who was called,
how many were being called, called out of what, and for
what purpose, I didn't know. Then, later, when Jesus was
killed, I figured that whatever kind of "called out assembly"
he had in mind died with him. Right? Wrong!

Shortly after Jesus was killed and buried we, who were
his followers, became aware that he was not dead! Somehow, he had overcome death and was present with us for
a number of days. In some ways he was the same; in some

ways he was different. But it *was* Jesus! His presence lifted our spirits and caused us to believe that God's rule in the world was going to become apparent to everyone in short order. Wrong again! After forty days of intermittent appearances, Jesus was taken from us for good, and once again our spirits were devastated. One of the last things he said to us was that we would receive the Holy Spirit. Terrific! I didn't know what that meant either. I had always believed in God. My Jewish heritage had prepared me for that. It had been a major shift for me just to acknowledge that somehow the eternal God was resident in Jesus. But to be told that there was still another dimension of God, a dimension called the Holy Spirit, blew my mind!

Ten days after Jesus' last appearance, we who were his closest associates, and some others, who also believed that he was the Messiah, were gathered together in a house in Jerusalem for a Jewish holiday. It was the day of Pentecost, a day of thanksgiving for the harvest, but also the day, fifty days after the Passover, when we commemorated God's giving of the Ten Commandments through Moses on Mount Sinai. We were Galilean peasants, away from home, in unfamiliar surroundings, in the city where our Lord had been killed. You can imagine that we were frightened, suspicious, cautious, and trying to be as inconspicuous as possible. We were grateful to have this place where we could meet safely, talk quietly, and pray. None of us knew what we were going to do next. I was all for returning to Galilee and getting back into the fishing business. Then, some things happened which changed everything; things which helped us to understand our mission, our group life, and God. Mostly, we began to understand God's Spirit, and how that Spirit works in our midst. Let me tell you about it.

For one thing, I learned that God's Spirit produces vitality. We were a defeated bunch, lacking direction and lacking motivation. While we were praying about what we should do, there was suddenly the sensation of a wind passing through the house. Maybe a wind had kicked up outside, I don't know, but as this wind passed through the room it excited all of us. It convinced us of God's presence, for in our language the word for "wind" and the word for "spirit" are the same. We, who had been struggling for days with Jesus' words about a spirit, began to connect the characteristics of wind with the characteristics of the Spirit of God. A wind is a dynamic force, almost unpredictable. You can't harness it, but if you raise a sail, it can propel you on your journey. It provides energy. So does God's Spirit. A wind is also a disturber of the way things are. If you have things all arranged one way, a wind can come up and completely rearrange things or put them in apparent disarray. We were to discover that God's Spirit sometimes unsettles all our settled opinions and sends us off in search of new patterns, whether they be patterns of worship, ideas about God, or ideas about how to conduct ourselves.

The next thing we were aware of was an aura around each of us that I would describe as a fire. Each of us was becoming so enthused that our faces lit up, and we were becoming inflamed with a newfound zeal. The notion of God's Spirit as a fire had an amazing significance for us. When God confronted Moses on the desert, he spoke through a burning bush. Fire had long been associated with purging, purifying, cleansing, refining, and getting rid of unworthy elements — so that what remains is of greater value and usefulness than it was before. What a picture of God's Spirit! Not simply coming into our midst, but resting upon us as individuals. The Spirit that had been in Jesus was now in us. His earthly body was no longer present with us. But we had become his body, or *parts* of it. If his Spirit was going to find expression in the world, it would be through us. We were being revitalized.

Another thing I learned from this experience is that God's Spirit promotes understanding and unity. You may recall that I said we were trying to be inconspicuous. We had gathered for quiet prayer, but as we experienced these new phenomena, one by one my colleagues became giddy, even frivolous, loud, and then positively ecstatic. We would urge one to keep it down, only to have another start up. Like a bunch of young children with the giggles, our expressions became irrepressible. Eventually, the sounds we were making didn't even appear to make sense. The whole room was filled with mirth. We had become "holy rollers." People out in the street began to gather in front of the house because of the strange loud noises coming from within. We were so taken with the experience that we tumbled out of windows and doors and carried on in the streets, every once in a while shouting, "Hallelujah, praise the Lord!"

Pretty soon, the street was filled with people attracted by this riotous display. Some couldn't understand a word of it. Others rolled their eyes and said, "Just a bunch of drunk Galilean peasants." But there were others, foreigners, who spoke other languages, who were infected by our enthusiasm. They claimed that they could understand what was being said. Whatever it was that we were doing, they could identify with us, and they got the message that we were praising God, even though their language was different from ours. It never happened just that way again, but it didn't need to. This one experience was symbolic of what God's Spirit was trying to accomplish: a breaking down of barriers.

When we thought about this later, it became apparent to us that this was God's way of reversing what had taken place so long ago in the story of the Tower of Babel. In that story, you may recall, humanity's language became confused, so that people no longer understood one another. The confusion came about because of pride and human sinfulness. Now the confusion had ended. Where God's Spirit was allowed to operate and was given free reign, people understood each other. There could be harmony instead of antagonism. There could be unity instead of division. God was making it possible for people to hear the message of his love in their own idiom. No need for everyone to be cut from the same cloth or cast in the same mold. The unity brought about by God allowed for individuality. There could be unity without demanding uniformity. Think how that has affected styles of worship! Some people are sedate, others are demonstrative. Some like lively songs, others prefer sober music. Some praise God loudly, others worship in silence. But the same Spirit gives utterance to all of us. The force that unites us is greater than the preferences that divide us.

I also learned that God's Spirit promotes change. Take me, Simon Barjona, a fisherman. I became Simon Peter, spokesman for the faith. I, who out of fear, had denied Jesus *three* times, was given the courage to stand before a crowd and convince them of the error of their ways. I, who was always putting my foot in my mouth, was now called upon to give a clear testimony about what was happening. Some people said that all this noise was evidence that we were drunk. I pointed out that it was only nine in the morning. Jews don't customarily eat or drink anything until after the first prayers are said in the temple, which is about nine o'clock, so we hadn't had time to become drunk.

Were we intoxicated, yes; under the influence, yes; we were under the influence and control of God's Spirit. That same Spirit brought to my mind a passage from the book of Joel that spoke of the last days. In vivid imagery the prophet had said, several hundred years before that God's Spirit would be poured out on all people. There would be prophesying, dreams, visions, and fire. That old expectation needed to be reexamined, re-interpreted, applied to this new situation. That is the case in every generation. God's Spirit is dynamic, not static. God is dependable, but his method of approaching us is flexible. The word God has given at any one time needs to be reinterpreted and re-appropriated for subsequent generations.

Change — that was going to be the hardest thing for us and for others to accept. It didn't come about easily. In fact, most of my people, the Jews, could not accept it. They never could accept the idea of Jesus as Messiah, and we eventually had to part company.

On the day of Pentecost that parting began. I seized the opportunity, created by our outpouring of spirit, not only to explain what was happening, but to indicate that Jesus was the long-awaited Messiah. I called people to repent of the actions which had led to Jesus' death and to become followers of Jesus Christ. To our amazement, 3,000 people became followers of Jesus that very day! The day before, we had been a tiny band of frightened Galileans. Suddenly, there was a large group of people looking to us for organization and instruction. Here was an assemblage of people "called out" of Israel. I began to understand what Jesus meant when he had spoken of his church, a "called-out assembly." In time, our expectations were again challenged, for we eventually discovered that our message was not simply for Jews, it was for everyone. Again, change was called for, and because some could not change, the church was divided.

What I've attempted to do here is to tell you a little bit about how the church came to be formed. As you have heard, the church is really the creation of God's Holy Spirit. As that Spirit is quite unpredictable, I don't think anyone can say what the church will be like from generation to generation. There will need to be testing, experimenting, adopting certain things for a while, and then discarding them when they are no longer useful. When God's Spirit meets human spirit, religion becomes personal, immediate, ultimate, and gripping, as it did for us that day. I do not know what God has in mind for the church. It will probably be a surprise for all of us. But whatever it is, God's Spirit will be in the middle of it. Therefore, let us expect lively expressions, accept differing attitudes, be prepared for change. They are evidences that God is working in our midst.

Paul at Athens:
The Apostle Paul

Acts 17:16-34

There are some things people don't like to talk about, because to talk about those things makes them feel uncomfortable. You notice that they are glad to talk about their victories, and you hear about those victories often. Their failures, on the other hand, are not referred to, because they want to forget them. By God's grace, I have had my share of victories. And I've also had my share of defeats. My name is Paul, called to be an apostle of Jesus Christ. When I talk about defeats, I don't mean just hard times. When I suffered as a witness to Christ, I was able to take that. What I'm talking about are those times when I really gave my all to a situation, and nothing, or very little came from it.

One particular experience stands out in my memory, an experience that I never alluded to or wrote about in my letters, and which probably wouldn't have been recorded at all, had it not been for my companion and biographer, Luke.

It happened in the city of Athens. I had been moving rather successfully through Asia Minor and Greece, experiencing some hostility to my message, but also seeing little Christian communities spring to life in response to the good news of God's love that I was preaching. I approached the city of Athens with some apprehension. It was a city that had declined from its former glory, but it was still a university city, and the intellectual center of the world. The question in my mind was, how I could get my simple message through to these philosophically minded people?

When I arrived in Athens, I went immediately to the Agora, the great marketplace, and I began to speak and to debate with anybody who would listen. I found the people there to be most attentive. In fact, that was part of the problem. The people were interested in every new idea that came along. In fact, it seemed to me, that they spent all of their time just listening to ideas but never acting on them. They lived on lectures. They had an intellectual curiosity, but they were loath to make decisions, to act on what they heard, to get personally involved.

In addition to being philosophically and intellectually sophisticated, I found that they were also a very religious people. In fact, there were idols and altars everywhere in the city. It has been said that there were more statues of gods in Athens than in all the rest of Greece put together. One of their own writers has said that in Athens "it was easier to meet a god than a man." I cannot say, however, that all of this evidence of religion was making any difference in their lives. Perhaps you know of cities where there are plenty of places of worship, but where precious little religion is practiced by the populace.

When I was invited to go to the Areopagus, an outdoor court room on Mars Hill, where Socrates had been found guilty of corrupting the morals of the city centuries before, I accepted. I was not being tried, you understand; it was simply that the Aeropagus provided a better atmosphere for lecture and debate than the open marketplace. I hoped that there I would have a better opportunity to get my message across. The experience was a failure, but I believe that we can learn from our failures. Indeed, if we open our minds, we can also learn from the failures of others. Therefore, I want to share my experience with you, in the hope that it will help you.

The first thing you should understand is the composition of the audience I was addressing. Some of them were Epicureans. They believed that there were indeed gods, but as far as they were concerned, those gods were remote from the world and uninterested in the affairs of humans. To them, the gods really didn't matter. They believed that everything in life happened by chance — that no one controlled destiny — neither gods, nor individuals. They felt that there was no providence. They believed that death was the end of everything, so that there was no accountability to anyone for how a person lived. Therefore, it is understandable that one of their primary teachings should be that the wise person will make the most of every opportunity for enjoyment within his reach. They believed that pleasure was the chief end of life, and this led some of them to the grossest kind of sensualism.

Can you identify such people in your day? They are people who say, "Of course, I believe in God," but then they go on living as though it doesn't matter that there is a God. These are people who live as though the only really important thing is how much they have, and how much pleasure they can experience in this life.

There were also Stoics in the audience. These people were of a more reflective nature. They extolled virtue and insisted on subjecting human passions to reason. They gave the impression of being above emotion, and, as a consequence, they appeared indifferent to both enjoyment and suffering. They felt that everything that happened was the will of God, so they tried not to care one way or the other what happened.

Do you know such people? They seem to be far more upright in their conduct than the Epicureans, because they are not seeking gratifications. But at the same time, they cast a pall of gloom over everything that might be enjoyable because they are expecting that every enjoyment has its compensating suffering. Such people are always uptight and they can never let themselves go.

Then, too, there were Jews in the audience, who were religious exclusivists. They were convinced that they knew God, but God was their God, and they were not particularly anxious to share their privileged position with others. I suppose you can still meet such people today. I don't mean Jews necessarily, but people from any religion who are confident that they have the only approach and that everyone else is lost. As far as they are concerned, God loves only *their* group and it is too bad about everyone else. I have discovered that attitude even among Christians, and it is all the more unforgivable there, because Christians ought to know better.

Finally, there were pagans in the audience. They were the most numerous. Some were following after this or that religious idea; others were completely devoid of any religious affiliation. Perhaps you have met such people. Some are seeking, but they don't know who or what they are seeking. Others are completely oblivious to any moral, ethical, or spiritual dimension in life.

So, if you have the opportunity to speak to these people, how would you approach such a mixed bag? What message would you try to get across?

That question brings me to the second thing that I want to do, and that is to share with you the gist of the message I delivered. I felt I needed some common ground on which to build, so I commended them for their religious interest. As I have indicated, there were altars and idols everywhere in the city. I acknowledged that this was evidence of a deep-seated desire to worship. It was an indication that they were not completely blind to the mystery of life.

That is probably true of any group of people, in any age. There is a certain amount of religion in all people, even though they may describe it more as wonder created by the growth of seeds, the birth of a baby, or the vastness of space. Even people who think of themselves as irreligious experience such feelings.

It was my intention, once I had captured their interest, to guide their religious instincts and aspirations to the proper object, which is God. Consequently, I had to move from religion-in-general to God-in-particular. I remembered that, as I had walked through the city, I found a particular altar with the inscription on it that read, "To an Unknown God." I was informed that centuries before, in 550 BC, a terrible pestilence had fallen on the city and nothing seemed to be able to stop it. Those ancient inhabitants felt that some god must be angry with them, but no one could say which god, so one of their seers suggested that a flock of sheep should be let loose in the city. Wherever a sheep lay down, that sheep was to be sacrificed at the nearest shrine. If there was no shrine, the sheep was to be sacrificed to an unknown god. That was how that particular altar I had seen had come to be established.

I referred to the existence of that altar in my opening remarks, for as I spoke to them about the altar to an unknown god, I said, "That God whom you worship in ignorance is the one whom I have come to proclaim." I wouldn't be surprised if such a statement could be addressed to any mixed gathering, even today. Probably there are many people across your nation who have no real knowledge of God. They worship occasionally, but they have no personal awareness of who or what it is that they worship.

Anyway, I managed to hook the interest of my audience right away, and I suppose I should have zeroed in immediately on my main message, which is the good news of God's love as shown in Jesus Christ. Instead, I allowed myself to be influenced by what I felt was the intellectual nature of my audience. I embarked on a very well-reasoned and philosophical discourse. I waxed eloquently about God being the creator of the universe. I went on to say that God must not be symbolized by statues made by humans. I told them that that creator God is also the God of history who takes an active role in the affairs of human beings, so that we are not the pawns of a blind fate that controls our destinies. I acknowledged that some people were groping for God, as though he were hidden by darkness. I assured such people that God is not remote from his world, and therefore, we don't have to grope in darkness. God is near to each of us. To make my point, I quoted one of their poets, Epimenides, who said of God, "In him we live and move and have our being."

For those religious exclusivists who were present, I reminded them of the poet, Aratus, who said that we are all God's children, and therefore none of us should feel superior to others. Having laid a foundation based on writers from their culture, I tried to build on it by stating that people were doing many things that weren't pleasing to God. I suggested that God had let this go on because of their ignorance, but the day of judgment was coming, perhaps in this life, perhaps in the next. I went on to say that I knew that there was a next life because God had raised a particular man from the dead. You see, I was trying to keep my remarks as general as possible, by not mentioning Jesus by name until the end of my argument. But that was a mistake. They didn't let me get to the end of my argument. When I mentioned the resurrection, they took exception to that idea, and as a result, they dismissed everything else I said. The meeting degenerated into a shouting match, and I had no further opportunity to speak.

I said earlier in my comments to you that I thought we could learn from our failures. I learned some things from my unsuccessful approach to the Athenians. I can best share what I learned by telling you how different people in the audience responded to my message.

First, there were those who scoffed. They said, "Who is this seed picker anyway — this distributor of bits and pieces of foreign ideas — that we should listen to him?" These are the people you encounter anywhere, who, when they disagree with an idea, ridicule the person presenting it, rather than opening their minds. I imagine that you can still encounter such closed-minded pseudo-intellectuals in your day. These are people who manage to avoid personal commitment by finding fault with minor points that don't affect the truth of what is being presented.

Then, there were the procrastinators. They didn't reject what was said, but neither did they accept it. Instead, they said, "Let's talk about this some more." Again, I suspect that there are still people around who respond just that way. They never get around to making a decision. I am sympathetic to those who are actively searching for truth, but there are those who spend their whole lives gathering evidence, without ever sorting through what they already know. Under the excuse of seeking the whole truth, they never get around to saying, "I can and I will affirm this much. I don't know everything, but I commit myself to what I do know." As a result of such an attitude, they never do get around to deciding on anything. I have discovered that you can spend the rest of your life in carefully considered arguments with such people and never bring them to a decision.

Then, finally, there were those who believed. There were not very many of these: Dyonisius, Damaris, and a couple of others, but that was all. I don't mean to belittle the fact that only a few believed, but in other communities, those who believed after hearing the message were far more numerous. What this experience taught me is that Christianity is not primarily a philosophy to be contrasted and compared with other philosophies. Rather, Christianity is a way of life, a way to which one commits oneself by a conscious act of the will, by a decision to follow Jesus Christ. Therefore, it cannot be put in general terms of ethics or philosophy and debated in textbooks or intellectual circles. It involves making a radical commitment of oneself to the lordship of a person, Jesus Christ, who is the Lord of life.

After the poor results of my presentation of Athens, I never again let myself get involved in a philosophical argument. I determined to know nothing but Jesus Christ and the power of his resurrection, and to give people the chance to decide to follow him. I have also stopped blaming myself when my preaching isn't met with success. I have learned that what happens when a preacher calls for people to follow Jesus Christ isn't all the responsibility of the preacher. Those who hear must be responsible for their own decisions. Therefore, I cannot close without giving you an opportunity to decide. Is there some decision that you should make today? Have you decided to follow Jesus Christ? If not, let today be the day when, through Christ, the unknown God becomes known to you.

The Providence of God:
Saint Augustine

Romans 13:11-14

I would like to say a word to all seekers of truth, and the word is this: "If you are honest in your search, it will bring you to God, for God *is* truth." But beware of what you call an "honest search," for in each of us, there seems to be an ambivalence; one side of us seeks to find God, but another side of us seeks to avoid him. That ambivalence is often hidden by what seems to be an earnest search, so that we convince ourselves and others that we really *are* seeking God and truth, when actually the manner of our search is preventing us from finding God and truth.

I can speak about that from personal experience, for much of my early life was spent in such a fruitless search. My name is Aurelius Augustine. Some people go so far as to call me Saint Augustine, but don't let that title fool you. I've learned that if one is a saint, it is not because he has lived such an upright life, but because God in God's grace, is generous and forgiving. I think some people call me a saint because I finally found that repose which I believe everyone of us seeks. However, I did not find that repose without experiencing a great deal of restlessness first. The summation of my own experience is the belief that God has made us for fellowship with himself, and our human hearts are restless until they find that repose in him. Let me tell you how God came into my life; perhaps it will help you to dismantle the barriers behind which you have been hiding, so that God can come into your life as well.

First, let me tell you about my early years. I was born in the year 354 AD in Thagaste, North Africa, in the province which is now known as Algeria. My parents were both

Roman citizens. My father was a pagan, who was not very considerate of my mother, nor very much concerned about how I conducted myself, just so long as I was successful in preparing for a vocation. My mother, Monica, was a pious Christian, a dutiful wife, and a devoted mother. She was the most significant influence in my life, though I often seemed to be doing my best to discount her influence. Some people call her Saint Monica, and when applied to her, the more traditional understanding of saint is appropriate. She was the finest woman I ever knew. From my birth she taught me the Christian faith, in hopes that I would one day choose it for myself. She taught me to believe in God, and she tried to impress upon me the importance of self-control, especially in the ruling of my passions, for this was the area that troubled me more than any other. She urged me to be virtuous, and yet she loved me when I was not.

As I look back on my youth, I can see how my character was developing in a manner which is common to most people who are given to self-centeredness and self-indulgence. Like most small children, I learned to demand what I wanted and to show temper if I didn't get it. I disobeyed my parents because I preferred to do what I wanted to do. As I grew up, I loved to play ball, not for the sport of it, but for the sense of conquest that came from winning. I was an intelligent child and an able talker. I often misused these gifts, either to get what I wanted or to cover my actions. I would sometimes steal, not from need, but for the thrill of getting away with something, or because a companion had said, "Let's go do it," and I was ashamed to suggest otherwise.

I tell you all this, not because these things were so terrible or so out of the ordinary, for in fact, they are rather typical of human development. The fact that such things are typical says to me that early in our development we start a certain trend, which can be called self-indulgence, and then that trend grows and finds greater expression as we grow.

Eventually, it becomes a barrier between ourselves and others, as well as between ourselves and God. In my life, this tendency was most especially revealed in the area of passion.

As a young man, I was consumed with desire. I did not wish to marry, for that might be detrimental to my schooling, so I simply lived with a woman. She was beneath my social station, poor thing, and would never be my wife. From her I took, but gave little. This is what I mean by self-indulgence — seeking one's own satisfactions with no concern for the cost to someone else. Our relationship lasted for many years, I taking love, but giving none. A son was born to us while I was a student in Carthage. I named him Adeodatus, "Gift of God," though I knew little about giving or about God.

In these and other ways that it now grieves me to recall, I spent my early years indulging myself under the pretext of gaining experience in searching for the truth. My style of life grieved my mother and often brought her to tears. In my heart I knew that I should be conducting myself better, but I refused to give heed to conscience. Indulging myself, I used others and kept God, in whom I said I believed, at arm's distance. The more licentious my conduct, the greater my sense of meaninglessness, and yet, the more fervently I indulged my passions to compensate for the lack of meaning.

It was while I was in Carthage, studying rhetoric, that I chanced to read a book by Cicero, titled *Hortensius*. I had chosen the book only to study the technique of this master orator. But as I read, I became impressed with the content of the book, and I was moved to begin a more earnest search for wisdom and truth. In itself, this determination was good, but I suffered under the illusion, common to many university students, that the intellect is everything.

I felt then that if the truth were to be found, it would be found by reason alone. This, I now confess, was another wall to keep God out of my life, for while God is truth, he is also love, and love is not experienced with the intellect, but with the emotions. I gave myself over to the study of philosophy. I even turned to the Bible, but I found its poor translation to be dull, compared with the keen intellect I found among the philosophers. Little did I know then what great truths I would one day find in the personal experiences that are recorded in the Bible.

I was captivated by the study of philosophy, but eventually I discovered that it was powerless to change me. It could point me to the truth, but it did not give me the power to become a truthful person. I desperately wanted to find God, but I wanted to find him my way, with my mind, not with my life. I wanted things to change, but I was afraid to change myself.

It was in this impasse that I became open to religion. But, as is so often the case with young adults, it could not be the religion of my parents. It had to be something I found for myself, and if that should upset my parents, so much the better. My father had died recently, but due to the winning example of my mother, he had died a Christian. My mother prayed daily that I, too, would become a Christian. Since Christianity was their religion, that was the one religion I could not consider.

Instead, I became attracted to an exotic cult called Manicheaism. This cult, which was very strong in North Africa at the time, promised to bring a person to God by pure and simple reason. The founder of this religion had attempted to combine Zoroastrianism, Buddhism, and Gnostic Christianity into one religion, which was then taught to be a form of Christianity. I became an enthusiastic follower of this religion and was affiliated with it for nine years. When I told my mother of it, she was more upset than if I had no religion at all, for she believed that accepting a half-truth often immunizes a person against that which is more truth. At first, she did not want to allow me even to live at home, hoping in that way to express her disapproval of my newly chosen religion. She pleaded tearfully with the pastor of her church to come and argue me out of my religion, but he, being a wise man, refused, saying argument would only confirm me in my position. When she cried all the more that I would be lost, he consoled her saying: "It is not possible that the son of these tears should perish." So she was reconciled to love me, if not my ideas, being comforted with the thought that God would one day deliver me from error.

As I look back on it, I am sure that one of the reasons I was attracted to that religion was that it demanded very little change. It did not disturb my personal life. I could continue to indulge my appetites as freely as I chose. It did not require me to accept much from the Bible. In fact, it denied the validity of much of the Bible. You see, I could consider myself a religious person, without having to change much of anything. I said that I was seeking light, but I was looking into darkness. This causes me to say that I have observed in myself and in others the tendency to use religion itself as a barrier to keep God out of our lives. Some choose an easy religion, because it demands little. Some choose a demanding religion, but become fanatical about peripheral matters. Some affiliate with a potentially helpful religion, but they remain peripheral themselves, and therefore, are safely immunized against letting it have any impact in their lives. They have their names on the rolls somewhere, but they have no personal involvement.

In my case, God in his graciousness allowed me the necessary time to extricate myself from that which never could satisfy. Many things this cult taught caused me to become skeptical. When I pointed out that science disagreed with some of their teachings, I was told to trust in the authority of the founder, Mani. When I said that I could not do that, they advised me to keep all my questions until one of their greatest teachers, Faustus, would visit, and he would answer all questions. When Faustus finally appeared, I listened to him, but it became apparent to me that this cult did not have all the answers they claimed to have. I decided to abandon the cult, though I held on to a general faith in God.

By now, in my thirtieth year, I had become a teacher of rhetoric of some reputation. I chose to go to Rome to teach. After spending a short time in Rome, I was given a position as teacher of rhetoric in Milan. My mother came to join me there, and as a result of her presence, I came under the influence of the bishop of that place whose name was Ambrose. At first, I went to church with her simply to listen to his eloquent style, for after all, speaking was my field. But I became increasingly impressed by what he had to say, even more than how he said it. He interpreted the Bible in such a refreshing way that, for the first time, the Bible became meaningful to me, and I felt that Christianity might be intellectually respectable after all.

I greatly admired Ambrose because of his intellect, his obvious learning, his devotion to his God, and his great love of people, including even me. Therefore, I consented to take instruction from him in the Christian faith. I admired Ambrose's ability to live a fulfilling and seemingly joyful life, in spite of the fact that he was an unmarried priest. It seemed to me that he had overcome the passions of the flesh in a way that would never be possible for me.

I was distressed by my own inability to control my desires. I thought that perhaps I should marry, and to that end I sent my live-in companion back to North Africa. But marriage with the right person did not present itself, and besides, I was afraid of its responsibilities and restrictions, so I simply took up with someone else. I could no longer avoid the fact that the real obstacle to my embracing Christianity and allowing God to enter my life was my own passion. The intellectual difficulties had disappeared, and I was face-to-face with my own weaknesses. Jesus was attractive, but my lust kept me from following him. My will was divided, and as a result, I was unhappy. I saw my whole life now as one ambiguous plea to God: "Give me chastity in temperance, only not yet."

Perhaps for you the problem is not lust, but something else you want to hold onto. You tell yourself that Christianity is unbelievable for this or that reason, and you half believe it. But your reason is only an excuse, so that you don't have to do business with God about what is really troubling you.

In my life, the stage was now set for God finally to get through to me. I had at last become honest about myself, but I was also unhappy. One day, while visiting a friend and telling him of my growing despair, I went out to walk in his garden. I was arguing with myself, saying on the one hand, "Why not decide now?" And on the other hand, "Can I give up all?" At that point, I heard the voice of a child playing a game in the next yard: "Take up and read. Take up and read." I took it as an omen, and going inside, I spied a copy of the Bible that I opened at random. My eyes fell at once on those words of the Apostle Paul that say: "Let us conduct ourselves properly, as people who live in the light of day; no orgies or drunkenness, no immorality or indecency, no fighting or jealousy. But take up the weapons of the Lord Jesus Christ and stop giving attention to your sinful nature, to satisfy its desires." Instantly, at the end of the sentence, serenity came into my heart and all the darkness of doubt passed away. I do not recommend that random approach to the Bible, but that day it worked for me. My heart and mind were now at peace, and I discovered that whatever strength we have comes, not from the negative approach, which says: "I must give this up," but from the positive approach that says: "I will follow Christ."

Soon after that, I gave up my teaching career and returned to North Africa, where I founded a small Christian cloister. Eventually, I was ordained to the priesthood, and a few years later, at the age of 41, I was appointed bishop of the city of Hippo. I don't mean to suggest that the ultimate Christian life is found in becoming a priest, or in living a celibate life. That was the direction my life took. What I want to get across is the idea that every one of us must decide for ourselves who is going to govern our lives: our passions or God. For parents burdened by the direction in which their grown children are going, I can only say this: love them, pray for them, and turn them over to God, for you cannot make their decisions for them. You are not responsible for their decisions. Take consolation from the thought that God loves them even more than you do.

Depending on Grace:
Martin Luther

Galatians 2:15-16

On a sultry day in July 1505, a university student was making his way along a road on the outskirts of the village of Stoternhiem in Saxony. As he approached the village, the sky became overcast. Suddenly, there was a shower and then a crashing storm. A bolt of lightning knocked the young man to the ground. Struggling to rise, he cried in terror, "Saint Anne, help me! I will become a monk!"

The man who thus called upon a saint was later to repudiate the cult of saints. The man who vowed to become a monk was later to renounce monasticism. I know, for I am that man. My name is Martin Luther. What happened in my life was later to shatter the structure of the medieval church and to make possible new expressions of Christianity. It occurred to me that it might be helpful to you if I described, from my point of view, the events that ultimately led to the establishment of the many Protestant denominations. But let me not get ahead of my story.

Perhaps the first thing for me to do is to give you a sketch of my early years and of the general way of life in Germany at the close of the fifteenth century. I was the first of seven children born to my parents. From the beginning, my father had great hopes for me; he had it in mind that I would become a lawyer, become wealthy, and care for him in his old age. My parents were reasonably pious Catholic folk, but with no consuming interest in religion. I was raised by them, and by the church, to know myself as a sinner, much in need of God's mercy. All of us were well aware of the nearness of the flames of hell. Hell was so real we could smell the sulphurous fumes, and we knew how close we were to the eternal punishment reserved for sinners. The only secure course was to lay hold of every help the church could offer: sacraments, pilgrimages, indulgences, and the intercession of saints. In fact, anyone who truly wanted to be assured of acceptance by God at the moment of death would do well to become a monk and withdraw from the sinfulness of this world.

I was often in depression, even after I left home as a student, for I was sure that my sins would condemn me. I studied philosophy and logic at several universities, receiving bachelor's and master's degrees in those fields. Then, in 1505, at the age of 21, I followed my father's wishes and began the study of law. It was that summer, as I was returning to school after a visit at home, that I had the experience I described earlier. That same year the black plague had hit the university town where I was living, and I couldn't help feeling that that plague was a sign of God's anger at me personally. Then, when the lightning bolt struck near me, I was convinced that God's patience with me had just about run out. It was for that reason I vowed to become a monk. My father was furious, and I wasn't particularly attracted to monastery life myself, but I felt obliged to keep my vow.

I entered an Augustinian monastery two weeks later. From the very beginning, the rigors of monastic life were laid before me. The head of the monastery asked me if I was ready to renounce self-will, to accept a scant diet, rough clothing, vigils by night, and labors by day, mortification of the flesh, the reproach of poverty, the shame of begging, and the distastefulness of the cloistered existence. I answered "Yes," and was put on a year's probation.

In 1507, having passed my probation, I was ordained a priest and celebrated my first mass. Then, and always thereafter, when I celebrated mass, I was terrified at the thought of addressing God, and I spent much of my time seeking purification and acceptance by God through mortification of the body, fasting, prayers, and confession by the hour. But nothing seemed to help; I felt no assurance of salvation, and my depressions were often acute.

While in the monastery, I came across a Latin Bible that I began studying. I was amazed to discover how much there was in the Bible that the people never heard. Most people could not read, and they depended upon the priests for instruction. One phrase kept recurring in both the Old and New Testaments; it read, "The righteous shall live by faith." How contrary that was to everything I had been taught! Somehow, that seemed to speak to me. I came to believe that it was faith — that is, trust in God — that God required, and not moral perfection, which I had been trying to attain. Perhaps there was hope for me after all.

Another experience that had a profound effect on me was a trip to the city of Rome — the holiest city of all. Here one could pray at a crypt containing the remains of forty popes and 76,000 martyrs. Here were kept the remains of the holy innocents slaughtered in Bethlehem. Here was the face of Christ on the napkin of Saint Veronica. Rome had the chains of Saint Paul, one of the coins paid to Judas, even parts of the bodies of Saint Peter and Saint Paul buried in several churches. Praying before any of these shrines carried with it great merit for getting some person out of purgatory. There was the *scala sancta,* the sacred stairway, which had stood in front of Pilate's palace when Jesus was condemned. Whoever crawled up those stairs on hands and knees repeating the "Our Father" for each step, could release a soul from purgatory. What dreams I had as I made my way to Rome.

But the Rome I found was altogether different. The priests were crude, boisterous, unlearned, superficial, and impious. The city, far from being sacred, was filled with crime: there were those who said that if there were a hell, it was under Rome. The church was filled with greed and corruption, from clergy to pope, and no one seemed concerned for Christian living. I stifled my disappointment and tried to tell myself that even though pope and clergy might be corrupt, still, holy church and all the departed saints held out the possibility of salvation. I myself climbed Pilate's stairs on hands and knees repeating the "Our Father" for each one, and kissing each step for good measure, in hopes of delivering some soul from purgatory. I regretted that my own parents were not yet dead and in purgatory, so that I might confer this blessing on them. Therefore, I resolved to release my grandfather by this exercise. When I reached the top of the stairs, the most I could say was, "Who knows whether it is so?" Doubt had crept into my mind concerning the pope and clergy. There was even a question as to the value of pious acts.

Following my return from Rome and further schooling, I received my doctor's degree and was sent to teach theology at the University of Wittenberg. It was here that my doubts and dissatisfactions grew stronger. At Wittenberg there were relics of numerous saints: a tooth of Saint Jerome, some hairs from the head of the blessed virgin, and 19,000 other objects of devotion. These were the property of the ruling prince, who charged a fee to all who wanted to come and worship there, on the assumption that such acts of merit might reduce the time they would spend in purgatory. It was becoming more and more difficult for me to believe that such acts were of any benefit.

During this time, I was also preparing and delivering lectures on the Psalms, Romans, and Galatians. The outstanding message of these books was the grace of God. That sentence, "The righteous shall live by faith," kept recurring. In time, the meaning of that verse became plain. I came to understand that my salvation depended on faith — on my trust in God — not on any kind of works or pious acts or merits granted to me by the church. It was the same for all people; any good thing we do is the *result* of salvation, not the *cause* of it. We are accepted by God as we are; we do not have to be perfect. It was the discovery of this truth that substantially reduced the depressions I had known all my life, and helped me to know the release of forgiveness.

You can imagine my consternation then, when in 1517, a priest by the name of Tetzel was given the authority to raise money in our vicinity by the sale of indulgences, that is, the remission of punishment in purgatory. You see, Pope Leo X needed money for the completion of Saint Peter's Basilica in Rome. It was announced, therefore, that anyone making a contribution to that cause would receive a certificate remitting a certain number of days or years of purgatorial punishment. Tetzel was so enthusiastic that he used to say, "As soon as the coin in the coffer clings, the soul out of purgatory springs."

I was outraged by such presumption on the part of the church. Therefore, on All Saints Day in 1517, I nailed to the church door 95 arguments I had developed against the sale of indulgences. My intention was to invite debate on the issue during the holiday festivities. I argued that the pope could remit only the penalties he imposed; I argued that indulgences bred a false sense of security; I argued that the pope did not have authority over purgatory. When no one showed up to debate, others had my arguments printed up and distributed throughout Germany. Tetzel read my arguments and published a rebuttal, at the same time charging that I was a heretic.

I took advantage of every opportunity to present my views and to defend them through lectures, pamphlets, even letters to the pope. I wrote to the pope, professing loyalty to scripture, to the doctrines of the fathers and the church, to the canons and decretals of the popes. At the same time, I said I believed I was at liberty to approve or disapprove the teachings of men. The pope summoned me to Rome to hear my cause. However, I did not want to have my case heard in Rome, for I questioned whether a simple German priest would find justice, or even a hearing, in an Italian setting. I appealed to my prince, and he prevailed upon the pope to permit my case to be heard in Germany. Cardinal Cajetan was to hear my case in Augsburg, but my initial interviews with him convinced me that I would surely be burned as a heretic if I stayed, so I fled to Wittenberg, inviting those who would interrogate me to come to me.

So it was that, some while later, I was required to come to Leipzig, a city nearer my home, to debate my stand with John Eck, a representative of the pope. He was an able debater, but instead of challenging what I said, he presented the views of John Hus, who had been condemned as a heretic and burned at the stake some years earlier. He then asked if I supported those views. I had to confess that Hus had not been entirely wrong and that, in fact, perhaps I had been a Hussite without knowing it. I affirmed that any articles of faith must come from scripture and not simply from the pope or church. In so speaking, I was required to break with the authority of the Roman church and to insist that the Bible, as interpreted by each individual, had greater authority than the church. Eck needed no further arguments to convince him that I was a heretic, and he so informed the pope.

The pope issued a statement saying, if I did not recant in sixty days, I would be excommunicated. The emperor had my books burned at Cologne. But, by this time, a number of princes and a considerable number of the people had come to agree with me. Therefore, in the presence of my students, I burned some books of canon law as well as the statement threatening my excommunication. The break with the pope was now complete.

John Eck was sent by the pope to require the emperor and the German princes to carry out the papal decree in Germany and to bind me over to the pope for punishment. I was called to a meeting of the nobility in Worms in 1521. I was told that there would be just two questions and that I could answer simply "yes" or "no." Eck had piled my books on a table. The first question was whether the books were mine. I acknowledged that they were. The second question was, "Do you repudiate your books and the errors they contain?" My reply was, "Since your majesty and your lordships desire a simple reply, I will answer as resolutely as I may, without doubting or sophistication, that unless I am convinced by scripture and plain reason — I do not accept the authority of popes and councils for they have contradicted each other — my conscience is captive to the word of God. I cannot, and I will not, recant anything, for to go against conscience is neither right nor safe. God help me. Amen."

The eventual outcome was obvious: I had already been condemned by the church; I would now be condemned by the state. Therefore, I left Worms and headed for home, even before the verdict was reached. And, as I expected, the verdict was against me. All subjects of the emperor were to refuse me hospitality, food, or drink. They were required to take me prisoner and turn me over to the emperor for punishment, for I was "a schismatic, an obstinate and notorious heretic." No one had the power to go against the emperor, but not everyone agreed with the edict. Having left Worms early, I was temporarily out of his hands, and by the providence of God, the emperor immediately became so involved in European politics that he could not see to the enforcement of his edict.

It was while I was on the road back to Wittenberg that I was descended upon by soldiers and taken prisoner. I thought the end had come. Instead, I was kidnapped and taken to the nearby deserted castle of Wartburg. It was then revealed to me that my captor was my old friend and my prince, Fredrick of Saxony. I was kept in the castle for ten months under an assumed name, and in the garb of a knight, so that no one would become suspicious and inform the emperor or my enemies.

The time went slowly for me at Wartburg, for I was not accustomed to confinement. Yet, during this time, I managed to write thirteen books and to translate the entire New Testament into German. That New Testament subsequently became the standard translation for all German-speaking Protestants.

But the time came when I could stay no longer. Things I was hearing began to distress me: indulgences were still being sold in Wittenberg and people calling themselves my followers were smashing statues, doing away with old forms and ceremonies, and getting ready to take up arms. As I disapproved of violence, I had to return to Wittenberg to bring the reforms under control.

Things that I had been thinking about and writing about now came to the surface. One of our Protestant practices came to involve me personally. We, who were seeking to reform the church, felt that the monastic life was contrary to the will of God. Consequently, many monks and nuns who agreed with us left the monasteries and proceeded to marry. We did what we could to help those nuns who left their convents to start new lives. Once we helped twelve nuns to leave a convent. Nine of them came to live in Wittenberg. I managed to make satisfactory arrangements for eight of them, but after two years, the ninth one, Katharina Von Bora, was still working as a domestic servant because there was no one to marry her. Something had to be done. She needed a husband. I must confess that I didn't love her then, but I asked her to marry me anyway. I felt that marriage would please my father, give him the heirs he sought, and give me the opportunity to set up the model of family life for the married priest. Poor Kate: her husband was an outcast, under sentence of death; there was little love and no money; her husband was 42 years old and had quite a paunch. It was a severe adjustment for both of us. Still, we grew to love each other in time, and had six children in nine years. How she put up with me, I do not know.

Our attempts at reform helped to formulate the characteristics of Protestants everywhere: the emphasis on salvation by faith; the emphasis on the supremacy of the Bible, rather than the teachings or traditions of men, in matters of faith; the belief that the scriptures and worship should be in the language of the people, and not in unintelligible Latin; the understanding that every believer is a priest, and that there is no superiority attached to the clergy; the understanding that every believer is competent to read and interpret the scriptures for himself. Actually, all we felt we were doing was rediscovering historic Christianity, as it had been before the corruptions added by humans.

Not only did our efforts have an effect upon Protestants, they effected the Roman church and all of society. For, when the Roman church felt the impact of our departure, the hierarchy began to take seriously the demand for reform, and took steps to put its own house in order. In the Protestant church, we found that when we gave lay people a voice in the church, it eventually led to a voice in government, which in turn influenced education, which in turn influenced discoveries, which in turn has had its effect on daily life.

All of this came about because, by the grace of God, a simple monk came to believe that we are made right with God, not through the good offices of the church, not by our own good works, but by putting our trust in almighty God. That is the message that I want to convey to you: not that God saved a German monk by the name of Martin Luther, but that God offers his salvation — his loving acceptance — to you. You simply have to reach out and receive it.

The Reformer of Geneva: John Calvin

Galatians 3:23-29

They call me a dictator! They say that I am power-hungry, arrogant, and vindictive. I pray that these criticisms are not true. I have repeatedly examined my own heart, and I am convinced that the only thing I have ever wanted to do was to be a servant of Jesus Christ and his church.

My name is John Calvin and by the grace of God I am called to help reform Christ's church in the city of Geneva. I ask you to listen to my story and to decide for yourself whether the things said about me are true. I am not seeking vindication, for I have acted according to the light given me, but I do hope, as you hear the things that I have to tell you, that you will gain a better understanding of how the Protestant church developed, and how much some people gave in order to pass it on to you.

I was born in Noyon, France, in 1509. My father, Gerard Calvin, was a layman, a kind of business manager for the Roman Catholic clergy of Noyon. My father had frequent disagreements with the clergy over business matters, but he nevertheless wanted me to become a priest. At the age of fourteen, I was sent to Paris to take my undergraduate training. The bad food and regimentation of student life ruined my health. I suffered from asthma and from frequent migraines. Nevertheless, I was a serious student, and I discovered that I loved seclusion and being alone with my thoughts. I received my bachelor's degree when I was eighteen and my master's degree when I was twenty. In the fashion of the day, I latinized my name to Calvin. As I was about to enter upon theological studies, my father had a serious falling out with the clergy of the Noyon and decided he did not want me to become a priest after all. "You should become a lawyer," he said, "for I have noticed how those who follow the law usually follow it to wealth." As a dutiful son, I left Paris and enrolled in the study of law at Orleans, and then at Bourges. I learned Greek, I read the classics, and I developed an open and inquiring mind. During this time I also met some young men who were Protestants, a term that was just becoming current. They convinced me of the importance of reforming the church, and I secretly identified myself with their cause, though I wanted to stay within the Roman Catholic church. Three years later my father died, and I was free to choose for myself what I would do with my life.

I returned to Paris, once again to take up theological studies, to write, and to receive my doctorate. While there, I met a fellow by the name of Nicholas Cop, rector of the university, and I discovered that he, too, favored the Reform movement. On November 1, 1533, sixteen years to the day after Luther had started the Reformation by nailing his arguments to a church door in Wittenburg, Nicholas Cop was to present an All-Saints Day sermon to the university. I collaborated with him, and it became an attack on the Paris theologians and an appeal for reform in the church. The theologians were furious. Cop was accused of being a heretic and had to flee for his life. I also barely escaped arrest, and had to flee Paris, for the King, Francis I, was loyal to the papacy and began rounding up Protestants and burning them at the stake as heretics.

I spent the next year traveling incognito throughout France, teaching Greek for a living, and receiving patronage and protection from the king's own sister, the Queen of Navarre, who welcomed Protestants. In Potiers I gathered a group of Protestants about me for simple worship and discussion. We met in a cave. That became the birthplace of

Reform worship in France. We served communion there, not as a mass, but as a memorial. It was becoming increasingly dangerous for me to be in France, so I began to look elsewhere. I wanted some time to think and to write.

I fled to Basle in 1535, burying myself in the academic life of the university there. Still, I received reports that Protestants were being captured in France, accused of heresy, and being burned at the stake. The king needed to be informed that Protestants were not heretics. I took it upon myself to write a small book about my new-found reformed beliefs. I titled it *Institutes of the Christian Religion*. In it, I attempted to set forth a Protestant understanding of the Christian faith that showed God in his majesty, Christ as prophet, priest, and king, the Holy Spirit is the giver of faith, the Bible as the final authority in religion, and the church is the people of God. I dedicated the book to Francis I and sent him a copy in hopes of reducing the persecutions which French Protestants were suffering. It did not help. The persecution continued. The king thought of himself as the hammer that would pulverize heretics. My book, which contained only six brief sections, has subsequently been expanded through many editions until it now contains 79 full chapters touching upon every aspect of the Christian faith.

Since it was unsafe to return to France, I decided to stay in Basle, where I could do what I liked best, writing and teaching in an undisturbed atmosphere. I wished to be a follower of Christ, but I wanted to do it in the agreeable setting of an academic community. I was reluctant to break with the church of my childhood, but I had no choice now. While I thought of myself as a writer, others saw me as a reformer. I had become a spokesman for the Reformed church — how much of a spokesman was soon to become evident.

On a trip to Strasbourg, which at that time was in Germany, in July 1536, I was forced to detour through the city of Geneva. I intended to spend the night and to be on my way. Geneva had only recently become a Protestant city, due largely to the efforts of William Farel, the pastor of the Reformed church. It may seem strange to you, but throughout Europe it was the princes who decided whether their countries should be Protestant or Catholic. Switzerland was divided into cities and cantons, each of which was governed by a democratically chosen council. Therefore, it seemed natural that in lieu of a prince, the council should decide whether the city should be Protestant or Catholic.

Somehow, Farel learned of my presence in the city that night and he came to me and insisted that I stay and help him with the work of reforming the Geneva church. I refused, saying that I was a scholar, not a man of action. By nature, I was shy, nervous, without force or courage. Farel countered by saying, "You are simply following your own wishes, and I declare in the name of almighty God that if you refuse to take part in the Lord's work in this church, God will curse the quiet life you want for your studies." I felt as though God from heaven had laid his hand on me to stop me and my course. I was so stricken with terror that I did not continue my journey.

My assignment was to be Farel's assistant, with special responsibility for teaching the scriptures. Geneva was a city of 13,000 people with three churches. There were three of us who were ministers, so there was much to do. It was evident that the city had become Protestant by decree, but that many of its people were not Christian by practice, for Geneva had long been known for its moral indifference. The city council felt that since the Reformed church was the established church, every citizen was a member of it by right.

We pastors felt that the Reformed church needed a constitution, so we drew one up which indicated that only confessing Christians should be considered members of the church, and that a confessing Christian was one who accepted the articles of faith of the Reformed church. After two years of preparation, the city council agreed to this. When the time came for communion to be served, we pastors said that we would serve communion only to those who had endorsed the statement of faith. The city council said that we must serve all who presented themselves. When we refused, the council met and ordered us to leave within three days. To me, the issues were clear. One issue was the necessity for discipline in the life of the church. The church has the responsibility to confront its members with a Christian lifestyle and to challenge those who are indifferent. The other issue was who should have authority over the life of the church, civil government or church officials. We pastors wanted to separate the church from the control of the civil authority. Geneva was not ready for these reforms, so we were expelled.

I returned to Basle, where I hoped once again to reassume my quiet life of study. It was not to be. Several Reformed pastors from Strasbourg urged me to come to their city and help them. When I refused, they reminded me of Jonah, who refused to do the Lord's bidding, and they indicated that I would suffer similar dire consequences if I did not go. I consented and became pastor and teacher to a congregation of French refugees who had been driven out of France by persecution.

Actually, the three years I spent in Strasbourg were the three happiest years of my life. In addition to my pastoral duties, I was able to write, producing an expanded version of the *Institutes*, a number of commentaries on the books of the Bible, and numerous treatises on the Christian faith. I also married at this time and had a very happy home life. I was invited to participate in a number of Roman Catholic-Protestant discussions under the sponsorship of Emperor Charles V, who hoped to halt the further division of Christianity. Through those discussions, I became acquainted with many leaders of the Reformation movement all over Europe, but alas, not only could we not agree with the Roman Catholics, we discovered that we could not even agree to unite as Protestant.

In the meantime, things were going badly in Geneva. The new ministers were too weak to stand up to the city council, the lives of the citizens were becoming more undisciplined, four of the city fathers were obliged to flee from the law, there were charges of immorality against the clergy, Romanists were attempting to win the city back to the Roman Catholic church, and some of the citizens were looking back longingly to the more sober days when Farel and I were present.

As it turned out, some people favorable to Farel were elected to the city council and they wanted us back. Farel visited me several times, attempting to persuade me to return with him. I told Farel that I would rather submit to death a hundred times than to that cross on which I had daily suffered a thousand deaths. In Strasbourg I was happy and useful. Why should I go to a place where I might be less useful and certainly unhappy? Farel then unfairly reminded me that if Geneva were a cross, it was our Lord who taught that we must take up our cross to follow him. In September 1541, I submitted, and we returned.

Upon our return to Geneva, I presented to the city council a series of ordinances which they adopted. The purpose of the ordinances was to place the discipline of the church in the hands of the church. A consistory, composed of the ministers and twelve elders, was to be responsible for the spiritual life of the members of the congregation, admonishing those whose lives were inconsistent with the gospel and refusing communion to those who would not repent. It was for this reason that people called me dictator, though I never was chairman of the consistory.

The issue came to a head when a notoriously loose person was denied communion by the consistory. He appealed to the city council that once again had a majority opposed to our reforms, and they granted him the right to communion. On the next Sunday, when communion was to be served, I preached that I did not recognize the authority of the city council in church matters, and that I was prepared to die rather than to defile the elements by serving someone who was under censure. The man did not come forward, and the church gained its independence.

There is one issue that keeps coming up, and I realize that I must address it. While I opposed the right of the city council to direct the church, it seemed perfectly appropriate to us that the civil authorities should punish those who violated the laws of God. If a person were guilty of breaking any of the Ten Commandments, whether against God or against one's neighbor, they should feel the weight of civil punishment. Heresy was one such event. Protestants were feeling the burden of that understanding all over Europe. They were being burned by the hundreds in Roman Catholic countries because they were presumed to be heretics.

A certain Michael Servetus, a brilliant Spanish fellow, who was a doctor, a lawyer, and a theologian, had written a book questioning the Trinity, infant baptism, and the authority of the Bible. This was heresy to Protestant and Catholic alike. He was brought to trial in France, found guilty of heresy, and condemned to be burned at the stake. Before the sentence could be carried out, however, he escaped from prison, and eventually showed up in Geneva, where he was recognized, imprisoned, and brought to trial. I was one of those who prosecuted the case against him, for I felt that his error must be rooted out. The city council could not decide on his guilt or innocence, so they asked for opinions from the councils of some of our sister cities. All of those councils agreed that Servetus was guilty of heresy and that he should die. Our own city council, therefore, found him guilty, and he was burned at the stake in October 1553. I tried unsuccessfully to soften the punishment, but I must acknowledge that I was involved in his death.

There you have my inconsistency. I denied the civil authorities the right to govern the church, but I was not above using the civil authorities to enforce the teachings of the church. At the time, I felt that I had to protect the truth of God, and the authority of the Bible. It was a terrible kind of authority, and I hope never to be called upon to use it again.

Now, what have I to leave behind that might endure when I am gone? For one thing, there is the academy that we started in Geneva, which eventually became the University of Geneva. Here we trained leaders who carried the Reformed church to many parts of Europe. In spite of persecution, the Reformed church in France grew to have hundreds of small congregations. We trained the pastors for those congregations. John Knox, a Scotsman, studied with us, and then took our ideas back to Scotland to start the Presbyterian church. Reformed churches also sprang up in Holland, Belgium, Poland, and Hungary. We were never able to unite them into one body, but we did manage to unite the Reformed churches of Switzerland into one body.

Through my writing of the *Institutes*, Protestants were given a clear and consistent theology. Through my commentaries they were helped to understand the message of the Bible.

Through our conflict with the city council, we were able to set a precedent for the separation of church and state. Even in our misapplication of the power of the state, as in the Servetus affair, we showed the dreadful abuses that can occur when the church is willing to use the power of the state to enforce its will.

I have always attempted to put the cause of Jesus Christ and his church first. As I have told you, that often went contrary to my own wishes. I can testify to this: when we put Christ first, we are given a strength that is not our own, and we can do things that we never dreamed possible. I do not know what God is calling you to do, but I'm sure that society and the church are always in need of reforming, and God calls on people like you and me to do it.

A Candle Burning Yet:
Hugh Latimer

Psalm 146

What did you expect to find in this prison cell today? Someone larger-than-life? Someone as articulate as Demosthenes, as robust as Sampson, or as fearless as Joshua? If so, you've come to the wrong place. Oh yes, there was a time when I was called "Hugh Latimer, the apostle to the English," and by that title people meant to characterize my qualities of leadership, vigor, and oratory. But now, I am an old man, sick, tired, and not always able to think clearly.

Why, only a few days ago, I was called before the court to give an accounting once again of all that I believe. I was too weak to speak. I prepared my remarks in advance, but no one would read them. "Recant," they said, "others have. Be reconciled with the pope and go free." No, that I could not do. Take back everything for which I had stood for, and go free? No. God will give me the capacity to endure whatever I must. I suffer from too many months in the confinement of this cold prison cell. But tomorrow all that will be taken care of. This old tent, this body in which I now live, will be offered up, and I shall be free indeed.

These past months in prison certainly have given me the opportunity to reflect. I have thought of my childhood, my Cambridge days, the ups and downs of life in the church. I've been a preacher in my time — a good one too — and I could preach again, if God would give me strength. But for now, indulge in the need of an old man to reminisce, and perhaps, from what I say, some good will come to you. You can trust the words of a dying preacher; I have no need to lie.

I think of my early life, and I'm impressed by how simple things seemed to be then. I was born in the little town of

Thurcaston, Leicestershire, in the last decade of the fifteenth century. My father was a farmer — not well-off, but able to send me to the university. I entered Cambridge University in 1506, taking my master's degree in 1514. I had, by then, decided to enter the priesthood of the Roman Catholic church, and I was ordained deacon in 1515.

During those years of theological preparation, religious studies in Europe were in ferment. Erasmus had developed a new text of the Greek New Testament that was calling into question the authority of our Latin Bible, and causing some students to favor the study of the Bible over the study of theology. Martin Luther's doctrine of justification by faith was causing others to question the adequacies of the ceremonies and teachings of the church as instruments of salvation. I was dismayed and angered at the freedom with which some of my colleagues proclaimed new doctrines. I denounced them and the "new learning" they espoused. I was as zealous in my persecution of the new learning as the young Saul of Tarsus had been zealous in his persecution of early Christians. Little did I realize that my life would follow a course similar to his.

The second thing you need to know about me is that my mind changed. Listening to my arguments against the Reformation was a fervent preacher of the new doctrines, whose name was Thomas Bilney. He apparently saw in me someone who was zealous, but without knowledge. Perhaps the very vehemence of my arguments convinced Bilney that I was really insecure about the positions I was defending. In any case, Bilney asked if he might come to me to make confession. His real purpose was to use the opportunity to instruct me in the new theology, and he led me to a rather sudden and intense conversion. I came to accept justification by faith and the authority of the Bible and to question the value of many of the rituals and ceremonies of the church. Inwardly, I became the very thing I had previously hated: a

Protestant. The more we talked, the more inflamed I became about such things as the sale of indulgences by the church, the abuses of religion, excessive devotion to saints and relics, and laxity in church discipline.

It was one thing to be inflamed and to speak quietly — it was another thing to speak openly. As university chaplain, I had the opportunity to speak, and I took advantage of it. I spoke against excessive devotion to saints, veneration of relics, and for the need for the Bible to be in the language of the people, for only the Latin Bible was authorized by the church.

My words offended the conservative churchmen at Cambridge and elsewhere. Because of my outspoken appeal for an English Bible, I was called before Cardinal Wolsey on charges of heresy, along with several others who had been distributing copies of the scriptures in English. The others were treated harshly and condemned for their activity. I was examined and only admonished for expressing my views. Though I was not found guilty of heresy, I became a marked man: someone who would be watched by the conservative element in the church.

The controversy continued with each side attacking the views and leaders of the other. When the arguments threatened to divide the university, the king's provost intervened and urged us to be more discreet. He did this at a time when my side had the advantage, and it was apparent to many that King Henry himself favored the reformers. If I had been a little more reflective and a little less zealous, perhaps I would have realized earlier that, even as I was acting from conscience, so were my opponents. Had we reacted with greater love and charity, we would have been less intent on destroying each other, and more intent on winning each other. But that was not to be. I saw the Roman Catholic church, and many of the trappings that went with it, as the enemy of true religion. And those who supported the Roman church felt that we who wanted to reform the church and make it English were the enemies of true religion. At the moment, it was we reformers who seemed to have the advantage of the king's favor, and we were not above using it.

What I would like to do next is to help you see how dangerous it is for individual conscience when the authority of the church is wedded to the power of the state. As I look back on it now, I should have been more wary of the support of the king. I should have paid greater attention to the admonition of the psalmist, who said, "Put not your trust in princes," for I was eventually to discover that the favor of the ruler is a sword that cuts two ways. If you think that you can use the state to further the interests of religion, do not be surprised if the state or the ruler have it in mind to use religion for the interests of the state. And once you have accepted an alliance between church and state because it favors your cause, do not be surprised that that alliance can also work against your cause. My own life has been a series of ups and downs brought about by the favor or the disfavor of one ruler or another. Let me share some of these happenings with you.

During the time of which I was speaking earlier, King Henry VIII was married to Catherine of Aragon, who happened to be his brother's childless widow. After some years of marriage, the king indicated that his conscience was now troubled, for he felt that this kind of relationship was contrary to scripture and to nature. He sought an annulment from Rome, but for political reasons, the pope was slow to act. The king, then referred his cause to the faculties of the universities of Europe, to see if they would support the king's contention. At Cambridge, I willingly took responsibility for securing faculty support for the king's cause, for it seemed to me that he was correct. When the issue ended in the king's favor, he showed his gratitude by inviting me to preach at Windsor Castle, and by making me his close confidant. Subsequently, the king rewarded me by appointing me rector of the parish in West Kingston. It felt good to bask in the favor of the king. It did not occur to me then that things could as easily go the other way.

I was convinced that the king was in a reforming mood. If those of us interested in reforming the church could find protection in the king's favor, all was well and good. Let me illustrate what that protection meant. Once, while visiting in London, I was prevailed upon to preach to the church there. I didn't have the permission of the bishop of London to preach, but I yielded to the pressure and preached anyway. I spoke against the necessity of pilgrimages and devotion to saints, and especially against the reliance by bishops on informants in the judgment of heretics. As I look back on it now, I'm sure that I was asked to preach by people who were my enemies, in order that I might be trapped. I was called to trial by the bishop of London on the charge of heresy. As was customary, I was already presumed guilty; the only question was the degree of guilt and the nature of the punishment. I insisted that I had not condemned Catholic doctrine or practices, but only their abuses. I was about to be excommunicated when someone in a position of power — I believe it was the king — applied pressure, and the charges were reduced. Before the trial was over, however, I was required to submit to an admission of heretical doctrines with no specifics mentioned. It was this charge that put me in future jeopardy, for while there might be forgiveness for a repentant heretic, if one were found guilty of heresy a second time, he would be burned at the stake.

I kept a low profile for about a year after that, grateful for the intervention of the king and unwilling to fall into the hands of those who opposed reform. In the meantime, the king, seeking to strengthen his position against the pope, required for leaders of the church to acknowledge the king as the sole protector and supreme head of the church and clergy of England. As far as we reformers were concerned, this was our declaration of independence from Rome. What we were not so willing to recognize then, was that the church was now deprived of independent action and had become subject to the state.

Taking advantage of what I felt to be the king's favor, I spoke out against the necessity of venerating saints, making pilgrimages, lighting candles, and so forth. I criticized the excessive veneration of Mary, the doctrine of purgatory, saying of masses for the dead, and the sale of indulgences. I urged people to give money for the relief of the poor and the sick, rather than to spend it on buying masses for the dead. But neither the people nor the king were ready for these latter reforms, and I was forbidden to preach for a time.

Again, this was but a temporary setback, for the king soon had new reasons for encouraging the reformers. In 1532, Thomas Cranmer was made Archbishop of Canterbury upon nomination of the king. Shortly thereafter, he declared the king's first marriage invalid, and Anne Boleyn, whom the king had privately married, was crowned queen. The pope, in turn, now declared that the first marriage was valid, and Henry began to fear possible attack from the papacy, the Holy Roman empire, and France. In seeking allies for a possible conflict, Henry turned to the Protestant princes of Germany, who had themselves only recently identified with the Reform movement. The German princes, however, felt that Henry was not a genuine reformer, only an opportunist. So, in order to improve his image abroad, Henry was quite willing to grant greater latitude to those of us who wished to reform the English church. I was given liberty to preach and was invited to preach at Court. I was appointed to be one of the king's chaplains, and in 1535, three other reform-minded clergy and I were elevated to the office of bishop.

What we reformers had long sought now seemed to be taking place. In the *Ten Articles of Religion*, adopted by the convocation, the basic doctrines of the faith were more clearly spelled out and abuses were corrected. The following year, the king set his seal of approval on the first authorized English Bible. Monasteries, which I felt to be the seed-beds of superstition, were being dissolved. Shrines and relics were being destroyed.

But, alas, all was not well with the Reformation. The closing of the monasteries became less an act of reform, and more an act of greed and avarice on the part of those who stood to receive the lands. Too often, those destroying shrines and relics were only interested in taking the gold associated with them. When I suggested that the priests might marry in order to correct sexual abuses, confession to a priest was unnecessary, and the body and blood of Jesus need not be thought to be present in the mass, it was too much for the king. Henry became increasingly disenchanted with the opinions of some of the more advanced reformers and required Parliament to pass "An Act Abolishing Diversity of Opinion," later called "The Six Articles." The sword was beginning to cut the other way.

In 1539, Thomas Cromwell, the vicar general, perhaps seeing his own days numbered, came to me privately and informed me that the king desired me to resign my bishopric. I did so, assuming that it was the king's request. Later, the king said that he had not requested my resignation. I do not know who was telling the truth, but the king made no effort to restore my office. In fact, my resignation was viewed as a protest against the policies of king and church — treason and heresy — and I was imprisoned for several months, daily expecting to hear that I have been sentenced to be burned at the stake, for this had already happened to many of the reformers. Later, I was released under a general pardon, but forbidden to preach or to come within ten miles of London.

I did my best to stay away from London, but in 1546 a tree fell on me, and I was obliged to go to London for medical help. While I was there, a friend of mine was being tried for heretical views, and I was requested to make a statement in his behalf. My own statement about what takes place in the mass came close to opposing the stated positions of king and church, and I was imprisoned again for eighteen months, this time in the tower. It appeared to me that my life was finished.

In January 1547, however, Henry VIII died, and was succeeded by his young son, Edward VI. Again, the fortunes of the Reformation were looking up. A number of other reformers and I were released from prison under a general pardon. Heresy laws were relaxed, and then repealed altogether, allowing greater freedom of opinion. Restrictions placed on the use of the English Bible were removed. I was invited to preach at court frequently and encouraged to preach throughout the realm on subjects which were important to me. I spoke against the sale of offices, personal immorality, public corruption, the bribing of judges, and the false embrace of reformed religion for the purpose of getting monastery lands. I spoke against certain agricultural policies which were strangling the poor farmers and driving them from the land. As far as we reformers were concerned, the sun was shining again, and we did not consider the possibility that the sun might set.

Then, in July 1553, Edward VI, the boy-king, died. Mary Tudor, an ardent Roman Catholic, was proclaimed queen. For her, Catholicism meant old doctrines, old liturgy, old ceremonials and customs, and these views were still shared by the majority of the people, for there is a conservatism, inherent in religion that causes people to favor the old and familiar. She also favored reconciliation with Rome. Under her guidance, the mass was restored, and England was returned to obedience to the pope.

The reformers, who had attacked the mass, were now faced with the choice of recanting their positions, going into exile, or remaining to face death. My friends urged me to flee to the continent. Others were doing so. Even the government seemed to prefer that we do that. But I was too old, too sick, and too tired to flee. Besides, I would be running away from everything for which I had stood.

I was brought before the Privy Council, found to be seditious, and sent to the tower, along with Nicholas Ridley and Thomas Cranmer, there to await further trial. Months later, we were brought to trial here in Oxford and urged to accept the Catholic position on the mass or face the consequences. When we refused, we were excommunicated and had every reason to expect swift execution. But it took a while for Parliament to re-enact the old statutes regarding the burning of heretics, so I have been waiting in this cold, damp cell for eighteen months. Ridley and I were examined again, just a few days ago. They urged us to recant, to be reconciled with the pope and go free. By the grace of God, Ridley and I have managed to hold up under it all. Now, they say, tomorrow is the day that we will be called upon to make a final sacrifice. May God grant that we give a good testimony to what we believe.

My reasons for telling you all of this are several. For one thing, I wanted you to be aware of the price paid by some for Protestant Christianity. I wanted you to see what happens when the power of the state is used to enforce the opinions of religion. May God forgive me for the times that I allowed that power to be used on my behalf. And finally, I want to encourage you to live by conscience. It will not be easy. You may suffer for it. But suffering for conscience's sake brings character to the individual, and in the long run, I believe that it brings justice to the nation and nobility to the race.

Epilogue

On October 16, 1555, Hugh Latimer, and his good friend, Nicholas Ridley were burned at the stake outside of Oxford, England. As the torch was applied and the flames mounted, Latimer spoke to his friend: "Be of good comfort, Master Ridley, and play the man. We shall this day light such a candle by God's grace in England as I trust shall never be put out."

A Brand Plucked from the Burning: John Wesley

Romans 5:1-5

In the year 1532, Henry VIII was King of England. He was married to Catherine of Aragon, whom he did not love. He was in love with Ann Boleyn and he wanted to marry her. He did all that he could to secure an annulment through the Roman church, but Catherine's nephew was emperor of the Holy Roman empire, and he applied pressure to see that the annulment was denied. Henry, however, was a man of great determination. He simply nationalized the Roman Catholic church in England and set up the Church of England, with himself as head of the church, rather than the pope.

Thus, there was born, full-grown, a new church with the same buildings, the same forms, the same clergy, but under new management. Elsewhere in Europe new churches were being formed by dedicated reformers, acting out of conscience, and their churches were genuinely reformed. In England, however, it was precious little reform, just new management.

Therefore, 200 years later, there were still some things in the Church of England that needed reforming, and by the grace of God, I was the one called upon to point that out. My name is John Wesley, priest of the Church of England, and founder of the Methodist Societies. I'd like to tell you how the Methodist movement got started and what I intended for it to be. To do that, I need to start at the beginning of my life.

I was born in Epworth, England, in 1703. My father was a priest in the Church of England. I was one of nineteen children to be born in my family. My mother was very well-organized, as any woman who had to care for so many children would have to be if she were to survive. It was from her that

I learned the necessity of a well-disciplined life, if one were to use his time as God intended.

My father was not popular with the people of Epworth, at least partly because he was a clergyman, and those people just didn't want a parson. They used to stab our cows and maim our sheep. One night, when I was six years old, they even set fire to the parsonage. My own escape from the burning building appeared so unlikely that when I was rescued, my father called me "a brand plucked from the burning." He made me feel that I had a destiny, and that I had been saved for a reason. My father stayed on at Epworth until the day he died, but I never cared much for those people after the fire.

Through the kindness of some wealthy friends, I was permitted to go on to school. At the age of seventeen, I entered Christ Church College at Oxford to prepare for the priesthood of the Church of England. I received my bachelor's and master's degrees and became a teaching fellow at the university for a time. I was ordained as a priest in 1728, and, as my father was having a hard time of it in Epworth, I consented to give up my teaching for a time and to become my father's assistant. Unfortunately, I always saw people as "souls" rather than as "persons," and as a consequence, I did not develop any warm relationships at Epworth. When my father offered to have me installed as the pastor at Epworth, I fled back to the safety of my books at Oxford.

In the meantime, my younger brother, Charles, had taken up his studies at Oxford. When I returned there, I found that he and several other students had formed a group for special devotion and study, which they called the "Holy Club." I joined their group, and because I was older than the others, I became its leader. I shared with them the manner in which I had structured my life, and my methodical manner of working. We encouraged one another in studies and in the religious life, fasted twice a week, went regularly to confession, and partook of communion once a week, things seldom done by the members of our church. Those who observed our habits called us "Methodists" — to them, a term of derision. We also did what we could to meet the needs of the poor, even though our own means were meager. I stopped getting my hair cut in order that I might save the money and use it for the poor, and from then on I wore my hair long. I discovered that while my income was thirty pounds a year I could live on 28 and give two to the poor. Later, my income was sixty pounds a year, and I could still live on 28, enabling me to give 32 to the poor. When my income was 120 pounds, I could still live on 28, and give 92 to the poor. It became a maxim in our Methodist societies later, that one should make all he can, save all he can, and give all he can. All in all, we were very pious and very concerned about the lot of our fellowmen, but still, something was missing.

Another incident which had considerable impact on my life was my stay in Georgia, when Georgia was still a British colony. My brother, Charles, had just graduated from Oxford and had been ordained as a priest. We both wanted to do something more exciting than to minister in parish churches in England, so we signed up to be missionaries. Charles was to be secretary to the founder of the Georgia colony, and I was to be missionary to the Indians and pastor to the colonists.

On the trip to America our ship was caught up in a hurricane, which I felt sure would sink the ship, and I was panic-struck. There was a group of simple German immigrants on board, Moravians by religion, who were calm and undisturbed even in the worst of it. I asked them if they were not in fear of drowning, and their answer was they were confident that they were in the hands of God. How I would have prized that kind of confidence! My own faith left a good deal to be desired.

When I met one of the Moravian leaders later in Georgia, I told him how their confidence has impressed me. He asked me pointedly, "Do you know Jesus Christ?" I answered, "I know him to be the Savior of the world." He responded, "True, but do you know that he saved you?" To that question, I had no answer.

I didn't get along well in Georgia. I had to pastor the settlers more than missionize the Indians. I had an unfortunate romance, in which I acted too slowly and consequently, lost the young lady to someone else. I preached sternly against sin and frivolity, and the settlers, who had a different view of life, were much opposed to me. The only good experience I had was the formation of a small group of people who met regularly for prayer, discussion, and singing. I didn't know it then, but I was setting up a model for such groups to be developed later all over England. That group helped me to see that I was too concerned with my own soul, and too unloving and unforgiving of others, but what to do about it?

I left Georgia a disillusioned man less than two years after having arrived, and I remember writing in my diary, "I went to America to convert the Indians, but who, oh who, shall convert me?"

It was in 1738, just a few weeks after I had returned from Georgia, that I was to find my answer. In the evening of May 24, I went unwillingly to a society meeting in Aldersgate Street, London, where someone was reading from Luther's preface to the Epistle to the Romans. About a quarter before nine, while the reader was describing the change that God works in the heart through faith in Christ, I felt my heart strangely warmed. I felt I did trust in Christ alone for salvation and an assurance was given me that he had taken away my sins, even mine, and saved me from the law of sin and death. I, who had been a teacher, preacher, and missionary, had not known what Christianity was until that evening.

I now had something to share. My brother, Charles, who had returned to England before me, had had a similar experience just a few days earlier, and we had all the zeal of newly converted Christians. It was here that we began to run into trouble. Neither of us had a church of his own, having just recently returned from the mission field. Therefore, we would preach in the churches of our colleagues. But one by one our colleagues became offended by our enthusiasm and we were not invited back.

A friend of ours, George Whitfield, had taken to preaching in the open fields, and he urged us to do the same. I could scarcely bring myself to such a possibility. All my life I had been so careful about decorum and order. I would have thought it a sin to save a soul outside the church and yet, for want of a place to preach, I submitted. I preached at a crossroads just outside the city of Bristol, and 3,000 people were there to hear. Thereafter, I preached every day of my life at a marketplace, a factory door, a crossroad, or a coal mine.

I averaged 5,000 miles a year and fifteen services a week, proclaiming the good news of God's love. Charles and I repeatedly covered England, Ireland, Scotland, and Wales. Our style was simple and quiet, not shouting. Though I must confess, on occasion I did shout. Once, when I was preaching in a church, I noticed that some of the congregation had gone to sleep. In the middle of a sentence I shouted "Fire." When the startled snoozers awoke and looked inquiring around, I finished the sentence, "Fire in hell for those who sleep under the preaching of the word." We reached the common people because we went where they were, outside the churches.

We related the Christian faith to social and political issues, but our attention to the poor became a threat to those who didn't want the poor to be aroused. Consequently, our meetings were frequently attacked by mobs and ruffians, who, in some cases, were actually hired by the local clergy. People's lives were changed, but there were those in the church who opposed what we were doing. Bishops of the Church of England said that we could not preach in a parish until we had received the permission of the local priest. With or without permission, I preached anyway, and when anyone came and asked me by what authority I was preaching there, I would say, "The world is my parish." Our purpose was to reform the nation, and more particularly the church, and to spread scriptural holiness over the land.

Charles, too, was a preacher, but more than that, he was a poet. He wrote 6,500 hymns that helped the Methodist people to sing their faith — Hymns like "Love Divine All Loves Excelling," and "Jesus Lover Of My Soul," and "O For A Thousand Tongues." The churchmen of our day were horrified, because Charles often set his songs to popular ditties, but at the same time, it meant that miners and workers could sing them easily, because they already knew the tunes.

If Charles' special gift was poetry, mine was organization. It became obvious to us that people who were responding to our message of God's love needed an opportunity for growth in the faith. We set up class meetings of about a dozen people each to provide for spiritual and moral growth, and for Christian fellowship. We taught people to read and write. We received offerings to help the poor. We set up a loan fund to help businessmen get started in business. We opened dispensaries and orphanages, then offered whatever care we could.

Groups of classes were organized into societies for better supervision. We imposed no opinions on our society members. All of us were simply seekers after holiness. Our philosophy was "Think and let think." One could belong to any church he chose, for our Methodist society was not a church. We did set up chapels and preaching houses for weekday worship, but we consciously avoided anything that would conflict with the services of the Church of England, for we felt that our movement was a part of that church, and we wanted to keep it that way.

Many laymen came to our attention, who had a gift for preaching. There was a limit to what Charles and I could accomplish as the only ordained clergymen in the movement, so we appointed these men as lay-preachers. They were not ordained, and therefore could not administer the sacraments of baptism and the Lord's Supper, but that was not necessary anyway, as our Methodist people were to receive the sacraments from the Church of England. Some of these preachers were eventually sent by me to Scotland and to the American colonies, as well as throughout England.

Charles and I determined that we would not leave the Church of England, but rather, attempt to reform it from within. Many of our preachers wanted to leave the Church of England, but we told them plainly, "Who leaves the Church of England leaves us." I was called Pope John by those who opposed my authority to appoint and remove Methodist preachers, but I knew my place; I was not a bishop. The Church of England only tolerated our presence, but since we did nothing contrary to sound doctrine, the church could not drive us out. However, things were taking shape in the American colonies that were to change our relationship to the Church of England. When the American Revolution broke out, most of the clergy of the Church of England in America returned to England, as did most of the Methodist lay-preachers. This left Anglicans and Methodists without a legitimate clergy.

Something had to be done to provide a legitimately ordained clergy for the Methodists in America. I found a Greek Orthodox bishop, who was willing to ordain our preachers, but the Church of England would not recognize such ordination. I pleaded with the Bishop of London to ordain some of my men, but he refused. There were some 15,000 Methodists in America, who could not receive the sacraments, and forty Methodist preachers who were not ordained and, therefore, could not administer the sacraments. The question of ordination may sound insignificant to you now, but it was important to us then. The Church of England taught that only a bishop could ordain a preacher, thereby making his ministry legitimate. It was further taught that there was an unbroken line of ordination going all the way back to the first bishop, who was said to be Peter. I did not believe that. In fact, my studies of the New Testament had convinced me that in the early church "bishop" and "preacher" were really the same. Therefore, I could conceive of myself as a scriptural bishop, and I could have ordained had I wanted to. The Methodists in America needed something, so in 1784 I consecrated one of my associates, Thomas Cook, and sent him to America as general superintendent of the work there.

The next thing I knew, the Methodists in America had separated from the Church of England, elected Coke and Francis Asbury as bishops, and established the Methodist Episcopal Church. Now Methodist preachers everywhere were demanding ordination, so they could function separately from the Church of England. The Church of England, however, had now found its excuse for being rid of us, for the church said, "Ordination means separation." My brother, Charles, who had been warning me for years that I was going too far, was beside himself. He even put his protest into a verse that said:

> How easily are bishops made,
> By man or woman whim.
> Wesley his hands on Coke hath laid,
> But who laid hands on him?

I never could call myself a bishop, even though, scripturally, I felt I had a right to.

Charles and I eventually patched of our differences, but we never could patch up the church. Perhaps that is the way it had to be. Perhaps the teaching of Jesus about new wine having to go into new wineskins applied to us. The established church was comfortable with the old ways; it served the gentry and overlooked the poor. Our message was not new, but it was more than the established church could take. We taught the necessity of personal conversion to God. We called for holiness and disciplined living. We were unconcerned about doctrinal differences, as long as each person held his opinions in love. We were concerned for the poor, the deprived, the prisoner, and the orphan.

It is from these roots that the Methodist church has grown. Whether it is true to its heritage today, I cannot say. Whatever it is, or is to become, is in the hands of its members. I hope that they will wrestle seriously with what it means to be the church in their time, as Charles and I wrestled with what it meant to be the church in our time.

Dr. Livingstone, I Presume: David Livingstone

Romans 10:13-15

Africa has taken its toll on me. I sense that this will be my last trek, but I'm not willing to give up. On this particular journey, we have crossed sun-baked areas that have burned the porters' feet, and we have slogged through rain and slush. There is little game to eat, and all of us are hungry. I myself have had to be carried for the past several days, as past fevers have weakened me. The natives have built this temporary hut for me right here on the shore of Lake Tanganyika, so that I might have some protection from the weather. Perhaps the Lord will give me enough strength to find the outlet of this lake that I believe to be the source of the Nile River, but if my strength does not hold up, I would like someone to know my story. Let me tell it to you.

My name is David Livingstone. I was born in Scotland in 1813. My parents were hard-working tenants living on someone else's estate. My family and I were Congregationalists, and I sometimes heard missionaries speak of their work in distant places. I longed to be of service. I was eventually able to save enough money to attend Glasgow University, where I studied medicine and theology. I applied to the London Missionary Society, and they accepted me as a missionary candidate. I received my medical diploma, became an ordained minister, and set sail for Cape Town, South Africa, in 1840. I was 27 years old. My great objective has always been to live like Jesus and imitate him as much as I could.

I made my way to the mission station at Kuruman on the edge of the Kalahari Desert. I felt that there were plenty of missionaries in the Cape Colony, so I sought permission from the mission board to go into the interior. I persuaded another missionary, Roger Edwards, to accompany me on a trek that eventually took us 700 miles into the interior. I spent months among the natives, immersing myself in their customs, laws, language, and idioms. In time, I was able to think like a native. I would gather people around campfires and tell them about Jesus. Word traveled among villages that I had medical skills, and people came great distances to be treated. They said they had heard about a white man who treated Africans like brothers. I bought a site for a mission station at Mobotsa by giving a chief a gun. We set up a dispensary, a school, and a preaching place. I frequently had to leave my work in order to chase lions away from our station. One of them, however, mauled me, and the bone healed badly. Since that time, I have experienced pain in my left arm whenever I lift it.

On one of my trips back to Kuruman I met Mary Moffat, the daughter of one of our missionary couples. We became attracted to each other and fell in love. I proposed, she accepted, and I hastened back to Mobotsa in order to build a permanent house for her. We were married and Mary joined me in building and maintaining the mission station. We built another mission station at Chonuone, where the chief became attracted to the Christian faith. He felt my methods of persuasion were too slow, however, and suggested that we should whip the people into belief. I had a hard time dissuading him.

We moved on to still another pioneer mission post where we were occupied with medical and evangelistic work. There we began to raise our family. We experienced a terrible drought that affected our food supply, so we were obliged to eat such things as locusts, roasted caterpillars, and frogs. We began to look for more favorable areas, but soon ran into Dutch settlers, called Boers, who did not want us to settle among them, because they feared that more British would follow.

A chief, who lived by Lake Ngami in the interior, heard that I was kind to Africans, so he sent an invitation for me to come to visit him. I sent my family back to Kuruman, because of the possibility that the Boers might attack while I was away. My porters and I eventually came to the lake. I was the first white person to see it. I felt that it would be possible to sustain a mission station there. I subsequently brought my family to the area, but the children became ill, and we had to return to our home base. We were discovering that Central Africa is a difficult place for white people to live.

In time, another chief invited us to visit him. I took my family to settle a station at a place called Makololo. I discovered some tribal people wearing brightly colored garments of printed cotton. Arab slave traders had made their way to the interior. The natives had received these goods by trading boys to the slave traders. Rather than give up their own children, the natives were trading young men they had captured in tribal warfare. I spoke against the practice, but the natives were very attracted to the colored cloth. Besides, they had no feelings for those they were trading into slavery.

In time, it was obvious that my children needed to go to Scotland to further their education. I sent them home in the company of their mother, who was not well and needed a change. I felt that I had to stay in Africa, even without my wife and children.

I returned to Makololo, where I contracted malaria. It has been a hindrance to me ever since. When I regained my strength, I set out to look for more healthful areas for mission stations. I kept looking for an outlet from the interior, either to the east or to the west coast. I felt that such a line of communication would make the mission enterprise possible, bring about legitimate trade, put an end to the slave traffic, and enable people to leave the swampy marshes and live in healthier localities. We headed toward the west along the Zambezi River. Villagers assisted us in every way that they could. I preached to them about peace and love. One tribe actually returned some women and children they had taken in a raid.

However, the closer we got to the west coast, the more suspicious the natives became. They had previously had encounters with slave traders and they questioned our motives. We began to see people being transported in iron chains. One chief offered me a slave girl and when I refused, he thought it was because she was too young, so he offered me another. I tried to point out to him the evils of the slave trade but he could not understand. Another chief surrounded us, threatening to plunder our goods. He demanded that we pay tribute: either a man, an ox, or a gun. All of these tribes tended to see their territories as sovereign countries, and therefore, they required tribute, just as countries in Europe require visas of all who want to travel through. I told the chief that we had come seeking peace, but he and his tribe found that hard to believe. I offered an ox, and they allowed us to pass. That is the way it went, village by village.

I was very ill with fever and dysentery. All of my bones were protruding. As we got nearer the coast, more and more of our porters became ill and disheartened by the cruel way we were being received. We barely made it to the Portuguese-controlled coastal area of Loanda. I was dejected and my mind was so fogged with illness that I sometimes couldn't even remember my name. We were well-received by the Portuguese and all of us were nursed back to health. This trip, which had taken six months, proved that it was possible to travel to and from the interior, even in the rainy season.

I began to wonder whether one could find a coastal connection by going east toward the Indian Ocean. We retraced our steps along the Zambezi. Dangers from animals were constant. At one place, I was charged by an angry buffalo that I had to shoot. At another place my boat was overturned by a hippo. Nevertheless, I was convinced that the interior was a great place to plant the Christian faith. The natives didn't seek the Christian faith, but neither did they oppose it. I was told about a great waterfall that we would pass. I could see the mist from it rising six miles away. I was the first white person to see it. I named it after our queen, Victoria. In village after village I proclaimed the love of God, and Jesus' message of peace and goodwill. The natives responded favorably. "That is what we want," they said. "We are tired of war." By the time I arrived at the eastern coast in May 1856, I had been on the road for four years. I hadn't heard from my family in three years. I boarded a ship bound for England and arrived home in December of that year.

News of my exploits had preceded me. My letters and reports had been widely circulated. Queen Victoria invited me for an interview. I was heralded as the man who had opened Central Africa. My emphasis had been on opening the continent to missionary enterprise, but others could see economic and political possibilities.

I spent time becoming acquainted with my family, engaging in speaking opportunities, and writing a book titled *Missionary Travels*, which was an instant success and produced a good income. The mission board wanted me to return to organize a mission stationed at Makololo, but I felt that my calling was to pioneer work, so we amiably severed ties.

I was offered the opportunity to lead an expedition, funded by the British government, for the exploration of Eastern and Central Africa. It would combine humanitarian, scientific, and commercial objectives. My wife and youngest sons accompanied me, but my wife became ill and was obliged to go to be with her parents at the mission station in Kuruman. It was a painful parting.

I hired a small paddlewheel steamer to explore the Zambezi and its tributaries. The boat was often in need of repair and was a detriment, but we wanted to see how far upstream one could go by steamer. At one place, suspicious natives on the shore began to rain arrows on our boat. I waded ashore, shouting in their language, "We come in peace." I told them about our love for Africans and our hatred of slavery, and they let us pass.

In September 1859, we discovered Lake Nyasa. The Universities Mission Board sent a group of missionaries to establish an outpost on Lake Nyasa. We took them as far as we could by steamer. When we arrived, we discovered tribes at war with each other, intent on taking prisoners, who would be sold as slaves. We encountered several caravans of manacled slaves. The slave traders fled when they saw our expedition, and we were able to free their prisoners. Some 19,000 people were being transported along these trails each year, 90% of them died along the way. When I asked chiefs why they cooperated with the slave traders, they said that the only way they could get manufactured goods was by trading human slaves. A man would sell for four yards of cloth, a woman for three, and a child for two. "How can we live without manufactured goods?" they asked." "The same way you did before you had manufactured goods," I would say. But, like people everywhere, they were not prepared to give up what they had become used to.

My wife was able to join us again as we looked for a suitable location for a mission station, but when missionaries from the interior reported that they had been attacked, we thought it best for the women to return to Scotland. My wife accompanied them to the seaport. Along the way, she became violently ill and died. I was brokenhearted.

Other members of our expedition became ill and had return to England. I was down for a month, but decided that I would stay. I then received word that the government had decided to recall the expedition. The slave trade, tribal conflict, and famine had decimated the villages. The government felt that white people should leave the interior. The Mission Board decided to abandon the mainland and transfer their efforts to Zanzibar. I, too, set sail for England, arriving home in July 1864.

Again, I spent time with my children, fulfilled speaking engagements, and wrote a book on the discoveries of our expedition. But I could not get rid of the memories of those helpless natives being marched to the coast to be sold as slaves. I felt that I had to return to Africa to fight that evil. In the meantime, the British government had found a new interest in learning about the watershed in the interior of Africa. They wanted to know the source of the Nile. They asked me to lead another expedition. I told them that I would do so only if they acknowledged that I was first a missionary and that I had to work in a way that would advance my missionary interests. The government agreed.

We set sail and arrived in Africa in January 1866. We set out for the interior with numerous farm animals, as we wanted to see if some of them would be resistant to the tsetse fly. We recruited natives to care for the animals, but they were so cruel and lazy that most of the animals died under their care. To lighten their loads, many porters threw away our supplies. Other porters, fearing the local natives, left their loads and fled. They carried the story back to the coast that I had been murdered. An expedition, sent out to determine the accuracy of the report, found it to be false.

As we moved further north, we found less and less food, and fewer people to trade with. We were hungry most of the time. We ate leaves and mushrooms to stay alive. We dreamed of food constantly. At night, various porters would drift away. One of them carried off our medicine box. With no medicine to fight fever and dysentery, I felt we had been given a death sentence.

In spite of incessant rain, fever, and unfriendly villages, we pressed on, finally arriving at Lake Tanganyika. I was the first white person to see it. Friendly natives welcomed us, and we made it our headquarters for many months while I searched the area for possible mission sites and looked for an outlet from the lake that might show us that it was the source of the Nile. I became increasingly ill with pneumonia and delirious with fever. I tried to get to the town of Ujiji, where supplies were waiting for us. At that point, a caravan of slave traders came by on their way to Ujiji, and they showed great kindness to me. They constructed a litter and had me carried by porters, delivering me safely in Ujiji. It troubled me greatly to be part of the slave caravan, and yet these people saved my life.

At Ujiji, when I recovered my health, I discovered that most of the supplies I had ordered had been plundered. Gathering what I could, I headed back to Lake Tanganyika. In the interior I came upon a market being held along the river bank. Some Arab traders got into an argument with natives that escalated into a slaughter. The Arabs were firing guns everywhere. The natives ran off in panic. Many jumped into the river and drowned. Villages were set on fire. Twenty-seven villages were destroyed; 350 natives were killed. It was like being in hell. I wrote up an account of the incident and sent it off to England. Public sentiment in England was aroused, and that led to the establishment of a royal commission to investigate the slave trade.

Meanwhile, back in Ujiji, the man who was responsible for my remaining supplies believed that I had died and sold off all of my bartering supplies at discount. He then invested the proceeds in, of all things, slaves. I was now destitute in the middle of Africa. I fell into depression. Soon thereafter, an expedition arrived at my encampment, led by a white man with an American flag. The man approached me and said, "Dr. Livingstone, I presume?" When I acknowledged who I was, he introduced himself as Henry M. Stanley, a journalist for the *New York Herald*, whose editor had commissioned him to come to Africa to find me, for there was a rumor that I might be dead. He brought letters and papers and told me that there were supplies waiting for me at a place called Tabora.

In time, my health was restored by good company and good food, and Stanley joined me in looking for an outlet from Lake Tanganyika. We could not find it. Stanley contracted a fever and we had to stop our exploration while he recovered. He then had to be carried on a litter. He urged me to return home, as he was about to do, but I told him that it was important that I find the source of the Nile. I sent a letter with him to the *New York Herald*, appealing to Americans, who had only recently ended slavery in their country, to do all in their power to end slavery everywhere.

Stanley has been gone for some months now, and I have returned to exploration of the shores of Lake Tanganyika. My poor body has been put through a great deal. I am sixty years old, but sometimes I feel as though I am a hundred. I have not accomplished all that I have sought to do, but I have attempted to be faithful to the Lord, who called me. Because of my explorations, many places have been opened to the gospel. As I see it, pioneer missionaries are only morning stars shining in the dark, but when we disappear, the light of the sun follows.

Epilogue

David Livingstone died on April 29, 1873, in a small hut on the shore of Lake Tanganyika while on his knees in prayer. His heart was buried there, but his body was returned to England and buried in Westminster Abbey. His grandson and granddaughter eventually established a mission station on the spot where he died.

God's General:
William Booth

Matthew 25:31-40

My name is William Booth. You may have heard of me in connection with the Salvation Army. When I was born, in 1829, England was involved in a revolution. It was called the Industrial Revolution. As in any war, there were casualties. People were cold, hungry, homeless, shoeless, and living in grinding poverty. Their misery caused them to sink even deeper into degradation.

My father first sent me to school, but as making a living became more difficult, he urged me to give up going to school and to take a position as a pawnbroker's apprentice. He said that by my work I could restore the family fortune — a fortune that had never existed. When my father died, I became the supporter of my mother and my two sisters. I realized that my livelihood depended on the misery of others who pawned what little they had in order to get money to buy food — or, as was often the case, to get money for drink so that they could forget their misery. Going to and from work I was moved to see children standing on street corners, begging for food. Though I worked twelve hours a day, six days a week, I knew I was fortunate to have any work at all.

It occurred to me when I was sixteen that politics would not cure what was wrong with England. Only religion could do that. I resolved that one day I would like to work in the area of religion. I worshiped on Sundays in a Methodist chapel, and at the age of seventeen I preached my first sermon to a small group in the church. I also began to preach on street corners, and as men would pass by, I would say, "Are you going to the pub to spend money that your wife needs to buy food for your family or shoes for your children?" It was a hard sell, and many people expressed their opposition, but some were saved. I invited some of these ragamuffins, drunks, and wife-beaters to come with me to church and to sit in the best seats, but this infuriated some of the chapel elders, who were simply not ready to receive such people. I began to question whether these Methodists had forgotten their humble beginnings.

When I was nineteen, I was dismissed by the owner of the pawnshop because I had served my apprenticeship and that meant that he would have to pay me more. I couldn't find any work in my hometown of Nottingham, so I set out for London where I was able to live with a sister and brother-in-law for a time. I got a job with a pawnbroker who allowed me one night and Sunday off. I attached myself to a Methodist chapel and preached wherever I could on Sundays. I set down a resolution for myself to pray and read four chapters from the Bible every day, to refrain from idle talk, to be humble, meek, and zealous for Christ. I sought to enter the ministry of the Methodist church, but they denied my request, suspecting that I might hold some heretical views with which they did not agree. A prominent shoe merchant by the name of Edward Rabbits had become a lay leader of a breakaway Methodist group called The Reformers, and Rabbits hired me from his own funds to become a full-time preacher in his group.

One day, a young woman, Catherine Mumford, a Bible teacher in another chapel, came to our chapel, heard me preach, and congratulated Rabbits on finding such a preacher. Rabbits was pleased and invited Catherine and me to lunch. We were immediately attracted to each other and I began to court her. After several months, it was clear that Rabbits wanted me at his beck and call. I wanted to be my own person, so I began looking for other places to serve. Catherine urged me to consider the Congregational church. I enrolled in their training school, but soon discovered that their Calvinistic doctrine of predestination was at odds with my desire to bring salvation to the least and the lost.

I took a preaching position with a group called Reformed Methodists, but they were some distance away, which meant that my romance with Catherine had to be carried on by mail. In time, I found the Reformed Methodist to be a disputatious sect, given to bickering.

Catherine persuaded me that I needed more education, for without it she felt I had no future. I joined another group called the Methodist New Connection and began taking theological classes with them. I continued preaching indoors and outdoors all the while I was attending classes, and because I felt such sympathy for the poor and downtrodden, many of them responded to the offer of salvation. The New Connection Methodists opened their hearts and chapels to these people and welcomed them. Indeed, they were so pleased with my work that they made me their number two preacher in London.

In 1855, when I was 26, Catherine and I were married. I completed my education, and as Methodists were inclined to do in those days, they assigned me to a different church in a different town each year. This kept me from doing what I really wanted to do, which was to be an evangelist. For ten years, we were traveling Gypsies, moving from place to place. Sometimes, I felt that the moves were a punishment, rather than a reward. During that time, the Lord blessed us with eight children. Catherine was occupied with raising the children, but even so, she began speaking to women's groups and found that she was well-suited to that work. Eventually, she felt prompted by the Holy Spirit to speak in church, and on an occasion when I was ill for an extended period, she preached in my place and brought people to tears and salvation. A woman preacher was a rarity in England in those days, and some people came to hear her because they thought of her as a side-show freak. God gave her a heart for the prostitutes of London, so she focused on that city, while I carried on my ministry in Cornwall. But my heart was burdened for the poor, the uneducated, the starving, and the lost. Catherine persuaded me to give up my work as a local church pastor and to come and preach to the poor in London.

I gave up my relationship with the Methodists and began to preach on the street corners of London's slums. One day I heard an evangelist preaching in a tent. When he asked people to give testimonies, I stood up and spoke. A short time later, people associated with a tent mission asked me to become their leader. I accepted, and with that, I found the freedom to do what I had long felt led to do.

Eventually, the tent collapsed, and we hired a dance hall in the area. That was the beginning of a policy of using the devil's domain and the devil's tunes for God's purposes. We called ourselves The Christian Mission. Wealthy Christians heard of our work and made contributions that kept us afloat. Catherine preached to the better-off people of West London as her health allowed, and that brought further support for our work. Every day we saw God at work, changing the worst of people into Christian men and women.

In 1869, we moved to a former beer house and made it our headquarters. From a soul-ruining establishment of the worst kind, we made a house of God, and a gate to heaven. After four years of preaching in London, I was superintending a permanent headquarters, a magazine, fourteen preaching stations, a number of soup kitchens, and 140 services each week.

A prizefighter by the name of Peter Monk was converted and he helped run our soup kitchens. A chimney sweep by the name of Elijah Cadman was converted, and he began to preach. One day, this Cadman fellow was preaching, and he referred to himself as being in the King's Army. He proclaimed King Jesus as the Commander-in-Chief. He referred to our evangelistic meetings as the bombardment and shelling of the neighborhood, and he introduced me as the General of the Hallelujah Army. I was impressed with Cadman's vocabulary, and I began to describe our work in military language.

When the next annual meeting of the Christian Mission was held, we called it a War Congress, and I spoke of having organized a Salvation Army. Some fishermen in the group thought that we should have a Salvation Navy. They put Salvation Army flags on their fishing boats and referred to me as Admiral Booth. I was presented with a steam yacht, but it ran aground and sank. Some horsemen even established a Salvation Cavalry. All of this, of course, developed interest in the press, and people came to the support of our work.

Always, where there is human need, people are inclined to focus on the salvaging of human wreckage by social programs but we insisted that we were first and foremost a salvation people. Our focus was on getting saved and keeping saved, and then getting somebody else saved, and then getting ourselves saved more and more, until full salvation on earth makes heaven within.

Catherine designed a uniform for women to wear in order to avoid showiness — no jewelry, no earrings, no stylish hairdos. My son, Bramwell, designed a bonnet for women and a uniform for men.

In 1878 the Fry family, a family of musicians, attached themselves to our movement, and developed a band with the intention, as they described it, to "jolly along the singing." I invited them to become part of my nightly preaching services, and from that point onward, spirited music became a part of our style. Other musicians joined them. They were unpaid, had to provide for their own uniforms and instruments, and had to agree neither to drink nor to smoke. We wanted them to demonstrate a style of life that would help people.

Not everyone welcomed our efforts. Since we were trying to redeem those most affected by alcohol, the brewers and pub owners felt threatened. They feared a loss of revenue if we were successful in turning people away from drink. They invited toughs and bullies to attack us. We were ridiculed as show-offs and goody-goodys. When these hired thugs fell upon us, it was often we who were jailed for disorderly conduct, for the police felt that we were provoking the attacks.

In 1884, 600 Salvationists went to prison in defense of their right to proclaim salvation in public. It was a difficult time for us. When my own son, Bramwell, was imprisoned, I remember writing in my diary: "Trying to make people good is indeed a weary, disheartening business. I wonder why God has not given up on the world long ago."

It was a difficult time for many in England. Poor people sold their young daughters to brothel-keepers, who turned them into prostitutes. We set up a shelter to care for those girls who were able to escape. In the first six months we harbored 84 girls. Those in government were unwilling to pass legislation to stop white slavery, so we started a campaign to pressure them to act. A newspaper editor joined in our efforts. To prove that such things were happening, we actually bought a thirteen-year-old girl and publicized the matter. The editor and another one of our people were actually sent to prison for being involved in the transaction, but laws were passed that eventually brought such business to an end. The publicity that followed brought our Salvation Army to the attention of all of England and the dominions. We have subsequently managed to open homes for the purpose of rescuing and rehabilitating young women in all parts of the world where we are active.

In 1890 my beloved Catherine was promoted to glory. She had been struggling with cancer for some time. When the doctors told her that her illness was terminal, she apologized to me that she would not be available to nurse me on my death-bed.

In this year of our Lord, 1912, I have now out-lived her by 22 years. What an impact she has had on our work! She was responsible for our policy of allowing women to supervise men — a startling idea in Victorian England. Because of her influence, we now stipulate that a woman can hold any position in the Salvation Army. When Catherine died, we did not fly our flags at half-staff. We felt that she had been promoted.

For myself, however, it was a dark time. Following Catherine's death I endeavored to assuage my grief by embarking on a crusade against social evil. I wrote two books titled *In Darkest England* and *The Way Out*, to show England a side of itself that England did not want to address. The books met with great success and the profits were put into a trust to help solve the problems that I mentioned in the books. It was my conviction that the only real solution to our problem was the personal regeneration of individuals through the power of God's Holy Spirit.

Critics said that I was looking for the millennium. I countered that I was simply seeking for poor human beings the standard of life that is provided for a London cab horse: shelter for the night, food for its stomach, and work allotted to it by which it can earn its food. The mayor of London announced that such misery did not exist. Our Salvationists rounded up 150 near-naked people, shivering in the cold on one bridge! We called for the establishment of shelters, hospitals, programs for feeding and clothing the destitute, factories for employment, aid for discharged prisoners, legal aid, and homes for alcohol abusers. We held out solutions to the problems of the poor, the homeless, the unemployed, and the prostitutes. In time, all of these issues were addressed by society. Church leaders, who at first opposed our work as meddlesome, eventually came to give us their support.

In these recent years I have traveled throughout the world visiting our work overseas. I have increasingly turned over the administration of our work to my son, Bramwell, who will no doubt succeed me. I had hoped that all of my children would be involved in the Army, but some of them have disagreed with Bramwell's policies and have left the work. My son, Ballington, was responsible for our work in America. When Bramwell wanted to reassign him, Ballington resigned from the Army and founded his own organization, Volunteers of America, with himself as general. These family differences have saddened me, but they have also contributed to an extension of God's work beyond the borders of our own organization and beyond the influence of my own family.

As I have been increasingly freed up from the day-to-day operation of the Army, I have had time to do that which I love — to serve as a roving evangelist, fulfilling my greatest passion, the winning of souls, for it has always been my contention that you can't make a person clean simply by washing his shirt, you have to do something about what is inside.

I am content. In recent years I have been losing my eyesight. Surgery doesn't seem to help. But God has kept me and blessed my life these 83 years. I sense that my promotion to glory is not far off. I am sure that our work will go on — that we shall witness to the saving grace of God through our Lord Jesus Christ, and that we shall continue to demonstrate God's love for the least and the lost in every society.

It is my hope that, having heard these things that I have told you, you will have better appreciation of where we Salvationists have come from and what we are attempting to do. Now, whenever you see our people going about their work, I hope that you will recognize them as brothers and sisters in Christ, who are seeking to make God's love real in a hurting world.

A Gentleman of Japan: Toyohiko Kagawa

Matthew 25:31-40

What would you say if given the opportunity to stand before your king and in one-half hour explain Christianity to him? And what if you had previously been taught that king was a god? I had such an opportunity. In 1946, I was called to appear before Emperor Hirohito to help him to understand the place of Christianity in Japan. I knew that I personally served the King of kings, but I could not help but be nervous as I stood before the ruler of my country who had always been known to us as a descendant of the Sun God. I was to speak with him for one-half hour. Instead, our conversation lasted for one and three-quarters hours. In the course of those remarks I said to him: "A ruler's sovereignty, your majesty, is in the hearts of his people. Only by service to others can a man, or a nation, be godlike." In closing, I pulled out my tattered Bible and read to the emperor: "Whoever would be great among you must be the servant of all." I do not know whether anyone had ever spoken to the emperor in such a manner before, but I was convinced that his needs were the same as those of the common people, and he needed to know of the importance of service.

How had it come to this point, that I, a commoner, should be standing before my emperor, attempting to instruct him? Plainly, I was there only by the grace of God. I would like to tell you about that grace and to share with you some of the things that God can do when we make ourselves available to him.

Nothing in my early life would have led anyone to think that I would one day be called upon to instruct a king in religion. My father was the owner of Kobe's principal shipping company. My mother was a geisha and his concubine. My father had left his wife and his mother to manage a small farm while he lived in the city. My father had five children with my mother, and you can imagine that we were not looked upon with favor by his wife. I was named Toyohiko after the god of a shrine not far from our family home. My family name, Kagawa, actually came from my father's wife. He had taken her name when he took control of her family fortune.

My father and mother died within two months of each other when I was but four years old, and I was sent to live with my father's wife and his mother. My life was made miserable by the two women, who naturally felt that I should be made to pay for my father's infidelity. I was bullied, half-starved, and made to feel like a slave. Feeling unloved and insecure, I concentrated on solitary pursuits, and as a result, I did well in school. I pleaded with my older brother, who eventually controlled the family fortune, to send me to school in a distant community. He agreed, and at the age of ten, I was enrolled in a boarding school in Tokushima.

That change was to have a profound effect on my life. Several of us students wanted to learn English, so we made contact with some American Presbyterian missionaries and asked them to teach us the language. Personally, I was a staunch Buddhist and had no intention of enquiring into their religion. The missionaries gave us copies of the gospel of Luke in English to read. The reading went slowly, but I was quite taken by the character of Jesus who loved people, especially the unhappy ones, for I was one of them.

My brother quickly squandered all the family money, so there was no more for school fees. I was taken into my uncle's family, who paid for me to continue in school. We students continued to meet with the missionaries, but since we read so slowly, Dr. Myers, one of the missionaries, told us the end of the gospel of Luke. I was moved by the death of Jesus, and in my heart I prayed, "Oh God, make me like Christ." I did not tell my uncle of my growing faith in Christ, for he was a Buddhist, and I felt he would disown me. When I was fifteen, Dr. Myers suggested that the time had come to openly confess my faith in Christ and be baptized. When I did so, I was amazed that my uncle simply shrugged his shoulders. Religion was not as important to him as I had thought.

Greater tests were to come. Japan was preparing for war with Russia and schoolboys were obliged to drill with a rifle. When I was required to report for drill, I refused to take the rifle, saying that I believed that it was wrong for Japan to go to war. The instructor knocked me down and kicked me in the face and stomach, but I could only hear Jesus' words demanding love for one's enemies. I was becoming a pacifist.

I began to accompany Dr. Myers on visits to the slums of Tokushima. It was a place that respectable citizens avoided. There I met a Christian man living by choice among the degraded slum dwellers in an effort to help them because he felt like that was what Christ would have done. He made a lasting impression on me.

My uncle wanted me to go to the university to prepare for a position in business or government. I told him that I intended to become a Christian minister. That was going too far, and this time he disowned me.

I went to the missionaries with my problem and they made arrangements for me to attend the Presbyterian College in Tokyo. Often I did not get along with the students. I felt there was much to learn, so I committed myself to read a book a day, a commitment I have tried to keep all through life, but this concentration on reading tended to isolate me from the students. I was a pacifist in a nation at war, and that was unpopular. I was called "traitor," "dirty Russian," and "enemy of the people." I worked with the underprivileged, and that didn't sit well with the students either, for the people I tried to help were often smelly and shabby.

I completed my college work in Tokyo at the age of nineteen and returned to Kobe to enroll in theological seminary. I started preaching in the out-of-doors, and the place I concentrated on was a slum area called Shinkawa, inhabited by criminals, pimps, vagabonds, and murderers — the off-scouring of society. For forty days I preached the love of Christ, but hardly anyone listened. Weakened by my own poverty and lack of food, I contracted tuberculosis and collapsed. I found an empty shack in a fishing village and stayed in it for months as I fought to regain my health. No one thought I would survive, but I did. Everyone avoided me because of the disease, except Dr. Myers, who came and stayed with me for four days, further illuminating for me the compassion of Christ. Though I was cured of the disease, it left me with weak lungs, from which I have suffered all the rest of my life. When I returned to seminary, I worked hard to make up for the year I had missed, but I was still disappointed that Christians not only refused involvement in the social problems of the day, but criticized me for being involved. I concluded that the ministry was not for me, and though I stayed in seminary, I decided not to seek ordination.

I did not know for sure what God would have me do, but on Christmas Day 1909, at the age of 21, I moved into the slum of Shinkawa. I moved my few clothes, pots, and mats into a vermin-infested, six-by-nine foot bamboo hut, which I was able to rent cheap because the former occupant had died in it, and people felt it was haunted. The smells of the slum alleys were so foul I wondered if I could last the night. There was one public water pipe and one toilet to serve a hundred people. Yet, I felt that if I were to win these people to Christ, I must live among them. Poor as I was, there were those who had no place to stay. A young man with a terrible skin disease asked if he might stay with me in my small hut, and I took him in. The next night an ex-convict asked for lodging. The next night an alcoholic. My peace was gone forever. As a student I received a stipend of ten yen per month. I worked as a chimney sweep for an additional eleven yen a month. This barely provided for a thin rice gruel, which I shared with my unfortunate roommates.

Life was now very demanding. Each morning I preached near the water pipe, then attended classes or swept chimneys, and at night tried to read or write, sometimes until two or three in the morning. I was known as "the preacher" or "the Christian," by the inhabitants of the slum. Some did not like what I was doing. One man tried to stab me, another set fire to my hut, another knocked me down, breaking four of my teeth. I was surrounded by drunkenness, prostitution, gambling, and cruelty. How I hated it all! How I longed to change it. Few were interested in my religion, but many sought my help. As I was able, I rented three more huts adjoining mine, took out the dividing walls and made a rather large hall. Here the outcasts, the poor, the down-and-out came seeking lodging. The hall eventually became a center of preaching, a Sunday school, a small dispensary, and occasional clinic. I was still not fully recovered from tuberculosis, and more than once I collapsed while preaching. From one of my lodgers I contracted an eye disease, trachoma, that made reading and writing more difficult and eventually robbed me of the sight of one eye. Even so, I continued to write and publish books of children's stories, Bible stories, and books on psychology. The income helped me to finance my work.

Once, when I was preaching in a book bindery, a young woman by the name of Haruko Shiba was present. She later began to come and hear me preach out-of-doors. She became a Christian and was baptized. We continued to see one another, and six months later, in May 1914, we were married.

I had nothing with which to provide for a honeymoon. We spent our wedding night in a hut filled with the unwanted, and the next morning she arose to prepare breakfast for fourteen of us. She made my work her own and our lives have been knitted together through all these years.

Some months later, through the generosity of some Christian friends and my seminary, I was able to go to America to study at Princeton University. While there, I was able to investigate living conditions in American slums and the kinds of social services provided. I was in America for two years. I received a Ph.D. degree from Princeton and returned to Japan with the conviction that it was not enough to minister to the people of the slums; the slums themselves must be changed. I had left Japan as a social worker; I was returning as a reformer.

When I returned to Japan, I felt that the poverty that caused the slums must be addressed. Though Japan was becoming industrialized through involvement in World War I, the workers were underpaid and forbidden by law to organize. I told Christian people that we had to force the government to allow workers to form unions. They said that politics was dirty and that involvement in it would bring the tiny Christian movement into disrepute. I felt that the church must not be a remote, pietistic cult divorced from the joyful and dirty business of living. Rather, it must champion the deprived. To make plain my close association with the church, I was ordained to the Christian ministry in 1917. I continued to exercise my ministry among the deprived inhabitants of Shinkawa.

I also became the founder of the Kobe branch of the Japanese Federation of Labor and began to build up its membership among the dockworkers. I guess I became a puzzlement to everyone: I was a minister without a church; I was a doctor of philosophy who preferred to run high school classes for laborers; I was a Christian who was critical of respectable Christianity; I was a pacifist who was prepared to stir up trouble; I was an activist at a time when officials were becoming concerned about trade unionists and communists. I published several novels and numerous poems about life in the slums and about the need for laborers to organize. My books became widely read, but because they challenged the way things were, I was also thought to be seditious.

In 1921, the dockworkers of Kobe went on strike. They surged down the alleys of Shinkawa calling, "Lead us, Kagawa! Lead us, Kagawa!" I promised to lead them if they would refrain from violence. They agreed, but the ship owners said the strike was illegal. I was beaten, imprisoned, held for thirteen days, and finally released. During this time the communists planned a mass demonstration in which they intended to destroy machinery at the shipyards. I just barely made it ahead of the mob to a small bridge which the massed laborers would have to cross to get to the shipyards. I urged them to disperse, which they did. The employers became convinced of the need for change, and the door was opened for the eventual legalizing of labor unions.

On September 1, 1923, a terrible natural catastrophe occurred. Half of Tokyo was flattened by an enormous earthquake. Five million people were made homeless; 100,000 people died; factories, roads, and communications were wiped out; hospitals were in ruins; food and water were unavailable; disease threatened. Through Christian friends, I set about to collect great mounds of food, clothing, and bedding, and by the grace of God, we were able to set up relief centers in and around Tokyo. The government took notice of what we were able to do and, though there were many who disagreed with things that I did or said, I was often asked to serve on government commissions dealing with economics, unemployment, labor, emigration, and welfare.

Somehow I could not stay away from conflict. I felt that the church was failing to proclaim the gospel of the cross of Christ. Too many Christians were what I would call "church-centered" and inclined to argue about doctrine. I called Christians to clothe the naked, feed the hungry, visit the prisoners, and share a cup of cold water. In their turn, fundamentalists said I was not evangelical enough; denominational leaders said I lacked loyalty. Often, I did not have the backing of the church. Yet I tried to use whatever gifts of literary skill, power of speech, money, contacts with people in high places, anything God gave, to help Japan's forty million underprivileged people.

I also got into trouble with the militarists who were preparing Japan for World War II. In 1931, Japan invaded Manchuria. While I was in China on a preaching mission, I apologized to the Chinese for what we had done. The militarists were furious; to apologize was to lose face. They saw me as an enemy. For the next few years I went everywhere I could in behalf of Christian internationalism, but it was my own country that declared war on China in 1937. My pacifism put me out of step with the massive non-Christian majority of my nation.

On a Sunday in 1940, members of the Japanese secret police sat in the back of my small church, listening to me preach on non-violence. I was arrested as a traitor, held in prison for eighteen days, and released with a fine. Christians were becoming suspect throughout Japan: we had ties with the west; we believed in democracy; we stressed liberty of conscience; we set loyalty to Christ higher than loyalty to state or emperor.

I had hoped that war with America could be avoided. I was even part of a goodwill mission to the United States in 1941. When I heard of the attack on Pearl Harbor, I was filled with shame. I could not cooperate with my government and did not support the war effort. When American bombs fell on Japanese cities, I condemned the Americans also for what they were doing. I made a speech calling on the American people to stop the bombing. The Japanese military propagandists doctored that speech for their own purposes. The war set back everything we had worked for: unions were abolished; our cooperatives were nationalized; our rural rehabilitation programs were scrapped; our social service centers were destroyed. The war was popular at the beginning because we experienced victory after victory. In spite of the fact that many in the government did not trust me, I was asked to head up the government's Wartime Relief Committee to deal with those made homeless by the bombings.

When, in August of 1945, America dropped its atomic bombs on Hiroshima and Nagasaki, the emperor announced that he had ordered all hostilities to cease. The war was over. Japan was defeated. There seemed nothing left to live for. Even the dead had died in vain. Difficult as it was for us to accept defeat, it was evident that dictatorship and autocracy were fully discredited. Japan was ready for democracy. The service, selflessness, and democracy I had for so long been trying to bring to Japan were suddenly the way Japan's leaders wanted to go. The prime minister himself called on me and said, "We need a new standard of ethics, like that of Jesus Christ... Jesus was able to love his enemies... I want you to help me to put the love of Jesus Christ into the hearts of our people." I was asked to help restore those reforms and institutions that had been dissolved or destroyed. I was asked to run for public office, but I didn't want Christianity to become identified with any one political party. Besides, I felt I must get back to my preaching. It was about this time that I was asked to speak with the emperor and we had that conversation I mentioned earlier.

I have told you these things, not to praise Kagawa, but to show you how God could use one person who attempted

185

to do God's will as he saw it. God has filled my life beyond belief, and I am humbly grateful. I do not know what God has in mind for you or for your country, but I am sure that God is at work in the world, and that he is at work through love. My formula for a rich and worthy life is this: Rule one: Give yourself, freely and without reserve, to the service of others. There is no rule two.

Between Alpha and Omega:
Tielhard de Chardin

Romans 8:18-25

When I actually held the few fragments of the ancient Peking Man in my hands, my heart leapt with excitement and a sense of fulfillment. I was holding the remains of the oldest known ancestor of the race! What had these creatures been like? What did they see? What did they think? Did our course of human development really pass through them? And what did these remains tell us about ourselves, and about our future? My career as a paleontologist, a student of antiquities, was at its zenith, and yet I found that my interests were moving more and more to the future.

My name is Tielhard de Chardin. If you have not heard of me, I would not be surprised, for paleontology is not a field with which the average person is well acquainted. I have written many books in the field, and if I do say so, I have become a respected scholar in the field of pre-history. But the things I am more interested to share have to deal with God and human destiny. I have written a great deal in this field also, but I've had great difficulty getting much of my work published. That difficulty is a part of my story, and I would like to tell you about it, because I feel that God has given me a vision, which can help you to understand this world of which we are a part.

I was born in 1881, in the Auvergne district of central France. I was the fourth of eleven children to be born to my parents. My father was a wealthy landowner, who was able to provide me with a good education. Even as a child, I was impressed with the ancient rock formations near my home, and I studied them with interest. At the age of eleven, I entered a Jesuit school some distance from my home. At the age of seventeen, I decided to enter the priesthood of the Roman Catholic church, and I became a novitiate in the Jesuit order. Still, I had an aptitude for the natural sciences, and all the rest of my life was to involve the worship of the God of creation, while at the same time exploring that creation.

In 1905, when I had finished my undergraduate training, my order sent me to Cairo to be a teacher of physics and chemistry. I spent much of my leisure time searching the desert for geological and paleontological specimens and speculating about the origin of the earth and the development of life. I became convinced of the truth of evolution. That may not sound like much of a conviction to you, but for one educated in the church in those days, it was quite a step, for the authorities in the church could not harmonize the process of evolution with the idea of God as creator.

After several years in Egypt I was recalled to Europe to finish my theological training, for I was not yet a priest. While studying theology in England, I maintained my interest in geology and paleontology that gave me the opportunity to participate in a number of digs and to increase my knowledge of pre-history. I was ordained a priest in 1912, but, because of my specialty, I was attached to the Museum of Natural History in Paris. I became convinced that there is a natural drift in evolution, which I attribute to the pressure of God, who seeks to push the creation in the direction of thought by favoring creatures with a larger brain.

During the First World War, I enlisted as a stretcher bearer, ministering to the wounded, working as a priest, and writing scientific and theological papers. After the war, I enrolled in the Sorbonne, and subsequently received my doctorate in geology, becoming a professor of geology at the Institute Catholic in 1922. It was in those years that I wrote an article urging Christian people to become open-minded about the idea of evolution. What I wrote apparently disturbed some of my superiors in the church, because they became concerned about my writings. For my part, I felt that I now had the credentials of a professional scientist that would enable me to show my colleagues that the search for truth, through scientific means, did not have to preclude the search through religion.

In 1923, I was invited to go to China to do research at a museum for geological and paleontological studies. It was a marvelous experience. I participated in numerous important digs and published a number of scientific papers. Still, I couldn't help asking myself what our discoveries said about the future of the race. What is our final goal? Where are we going? What is God's place in all of this? If we have the capacity to think, doesn't that mean that the potential must have been there at the beginning of the process of evolution? If we are the product of evolution, when was the particular moment when life became human? I wrote about these questions, too, and addressed them in my classroom. The students, a part of that lost generation of the '20s, were enthusiastic about my approach, but my superiors in the Jesuit Order thought that some questions were better not asked and some answers better not given. Feeling that my probing of these issues might undermine the faith of others, my superiors refused to grant me the permission I needed as a member of my Order to publish what they called my most speculative writings. They urged me to return to China and to limit my writings to the area of my scientific expertise — the past.

I had, in effect, been exiled to China. Still, it was the place where my research into the pre-history of the race could be carried on without inhibition. In 1927, I wrote a book of personal observations about the nature of God and creation, which I titled, *The Divine Mileau*. It was my contention that the mileau into which each of us is born, is God. God is omnipresent. God reveals himself in everything. Everything proceeds from its beginning in God, which we could call the Alpha or beginning point, and is proceeding inevitably toward its culmination in God, which I called the Omega point. My contention was that the ultimate stuff of the universe was, therefore, not matter, but spirit, or mind, and that some of that ultimate stuff must be present in everything.

I saw myself as an apostle to science, who was attempting to open the minds of scientific people to the spiritual side of life. I tried to use Christian language, but my superiors felt that I gave too much comfort to humanists and agnostics. They felt that what I was proclaiming was pantheism, the notion that God is a combination of everything that exists. My superiors refused to give me permission to publish the book, and therefore, I was unable to secure permission for the publication of many of my pamphlets and articles. I did circulate many of my works among colleagues in mimeographed form. Some colleagues urged me to leave my Order, indeed, to leave the church, if necessary, but I saw myself as a priest fully as much as a scientist. I had taken a vow of obedience, and I had to be obedient, even in disagreement. I accepted their opinions as the will of God. Perhaps my ideas were too much in advance of my time. Still, I believed that if my ideas contained truth, they would inevitably be accepted, for I believe that our destiny beckons us toward the truth.

I immersed myself in my work and had the good fortune to become involved in the work that led to the discovery of the Peking Man, one of the forerunners of our present human race. That discovery, and my subsequent writings about it, confirmed my place as an international authority on pre-history, but, as I said at the beginning of my remarks, my ideas ran more to the future than to the past. I felt that there would be no future for humanity without science, but that there would be no future for science without religion to inspire it. I was most interested to bring about a synthesis of science and religion that would contribute to the advancement of the race. If there is no spiritual side to life, then life is meaningless and absurd. As an authority in my field, I was called upon to participate in projects all around the world. I traveled to places such as Mongolia, Burma, Java, India, Africa, and frequently to Europe and the United States. Always, I was asking myself, what is the common thread that binds the diverse peoples of the earth together, and where is it taking us? Unfortunately, I didn't have time to put my thoughts down in a consistent manner.

In 1939, I was caught in the war in China, unable to leave or to carry on my work, so I finally had the opportunity to put my thoughts on paper. I wrote a book titled *The Phenomenon of Man*. In it, I contended that evolution is a curve that everything must follow. Whereas most scientists see evolution as a random process, without direction, I saw it as a directed process from matter to life and thought; from simplicity to complexity; from chaos to order. Always, it is directed by God. Creation is moving inexorably in the direction of consciousness. The human race is the most advanced frontier of that creation. Indeed, we are the summit of the new creation, for at some point in the evolution of life, we began to think, and that, I take it, was the moment of the creation of the human race, the moment that is recorded for us in story form in the story of the Garden of Eden. It is toward the development of thought, the spiritual dimension of creation, that evolution is carrying us. That which increases our spiritual growth will survive; that which settles for the material will disappear into oblivion like so many species before us. The created world has sprung from the mind of God; it is toward union with that mind that we are now evolving. There may be numerous branches off the main stem, as life probes for its destiny, but we humans are at the head of the main stem.

At the deepest level of each individual, there is a desperate longing for something infinite. That is what the psalmist felt when he cried out, "My soul thirsts for God, for the living God." We are more than just matter. We have a soul. That is why, when I held the remnants of Peking Man in my hand, I was not satisfied to reflect on our human past. That ancient cousin was part of our struggle toward our destiny. Did he know it? Did he feel it? Whether he did or not, you and I are a part of his fulfillment. God is beckoning us toward our omega point in which everything will converge and find its importance. It is about that convergence that Paul speaks mystically when he says that we are Christ's, Christ is God's, and God will be all in all. I do not understand it myself, but I think that we are moving toward an ultimate union with God, in which we shall keep our individuality and yet be associated with God.

The power of that beckoning, that affinity, is love. In the scriptures we are told that God is love. Not simply that God *loves,* but that God *is* love. I would submit that that force, which draws us toward our destiny, is love. Similarly, that force which attracts atoms and molecules to one another that binds matter together, as well as conscious souls, can be called love. That is the force that welds individuals together without destroying their personalities. Love is the agent that binds us together and gives the world its shape. Therefore, I am basically optimistic about life. There is a fundamental oneness in the human family, which will succeed in bringing us together. The wars which threaten us will eventually die out as we learn to cooperate with the force of love, which will ultimately reconcile us to God and to one another. For me, all of this fits into the framework of the Christian faith, for I see Christ as a guide, a model, a trainer who has come from God to point out the way of love. Christ has become the forerunner of the new human being we are called to become. By following his way of love, we shall find the destiny toward which we are moving.

When I finished the book that I considered to be a defense of the Christian position, my superiors again denied me permission to publish it. Indeed, the refusal seemed to come from unnamed persons inside the Vatican itself. I have been trying ever since to overcome their concerns, but without success. I may not see my books published during my lifetime, but I hope that there is enough truth in them that eventually they may be read by people whose minds will be expanded by what I had to say.

I was able to leave China in 1941, and to make my way to the United States, where I carried on further research during the Second World War. Following the War, I returned to Paris, where I was often a speaker at conferences, but my superiors wanted to be certain that there would be no repetition of the influence I have had on Parisian students after the First War, so they refused to allow my name to go forward for a chair at the College de France. In fact, they insisted that I leave Paris. So it was that at the age of seventy, I once again became an exile from my beloved France.

I have prayed to God to keep me from bitterness and God has answered my prayers. I have been able to continue my work in the United States. I have been able to publish articles in my field. I have been given a vision of what I believe to be the destiny of the race. I have been able to serve God and humanity as a priest and as an explorer of the forward edge of human knowledge.

And what are the lessons that I can share with you? For one thing, I urge you not to lose heart when there is opposition. Our Lord had to go to a cross. But there was a resurrection. Again, I urge you to be open-minded toward those who may differ with you. God may have chosen the person with the strangest ideas to bring you a word you need to hear. How I wish the church had allowed me a wider audience. If I am wrong, I could have been corrected by dialogue. If I am right, others might have benefited. And one more thing, don't be afraid to use your imagination and to think about connections. Who would ever think that an old bone-digger such as I, could even find hope for the future while rummaging around in humanity's past? Moreover, I urge you to approach the world reverently. It is a revelation of the grandeur of God. Increasingly, for me the study of God's world has become an experience akin to worship. And finally, let love find its expression through your life. Love is the energy that propels us between the alpha of our beginning and the omega of our completion. It is the power that makes us one.

An American Prophet:
Walter Rauschenbusch

Amos 5:11-12, 14-15, 21-24

I was brought up in a preacher's family, but I was never taught that Christianity had any social responsibility. I had a religious experience when I was seventeen, but I never thought about the social expression of my faith. I was ordained for the Christian ministry at the age of 25, but no one told me that that would involve more than saving souls. I went to my first ministerial assignment in the tenement jungle of New York City and there God began my social education. I lived daily with people who knew grinding poverty. I saw its effects in the form of insecurity, malnutrition, wasted lives, alcoholism, hopelessness, crime, and disease. It changed me forever and convinced me that something was wrong with our current economic system. I could not keep quiet about it, and therefore God used me to ignite a fire for social justice, the consequences of which are still being felt in our society. My name is Walter Rauschenbusch. I'd like to tell you my story, for I think God gave me some ideas for Christian living that might help you.

I was born in Rochester, New York, in 1861. My parents had moved there from Germany in 1854. My father was a Baptist minister who came to this country to work among German immigrants as a pastor, author, and educator. He served on the faculty of Rochester Baptist Theological Seminary in its German Department. For six generations our family had produced Christian ministers and I suppose I knew from the beginning that I was to be the seventh generation. But like every preacher's kid, I had to assert my individuality. If there was devilment, I was the leader. I was admired among my peers for my ability to use profanity. On occasions, my father threatened to expel me from Sunday school because he thought my independent judgments in matters of religion bordered on the heretical.

Nevertheless, when I was seventeen, God got through to me and I had a profound religious experience that convinced me of the reality of God. I no longer resisted the ministry. In fact, I went to Germany to prepare for it and stayed there for several years. I mastered German, Greek, and Latin. When I returned to the States, I was so enthusiastic that I took my senior year in college and my first year of theological seminary at the same time. While in seminary, I came to the conclusion that whatever one believes is of little consequence if it is not put into practice, so I made a commitment to try to follow Christ in my daily life. Still, I was not sure how that might be carried out. I received my theological degree from Rochester Theological Seminary in 1886. I was 25 years old and anxious to go to India as a missionary, but the mission society felt that I needed some years of pastoral experience first. I didn't know it then, but there was plenty to do in this country.

I accepted a position as pastor of the Second German Baptist Church of New York City that same year. The church was situated on West 42nd Street, in a tough neighborhood known as Hell's Kitchen. I was depressed by what I saw and appalled at the neighborhood. As a preacher's family, we had never been rich, but we had never been poor either. Here was poverty and squalor at its worst. Every day, I saw how hunger, cold, and misery drove people to theft, brutality, and decadence. It was apparent also that no one was doing anything about it. I had come to save souls, but who was going to save bodies? The church could not meet the needs of these people. Only the government had the resources. I felt that it was the duty of the church to see that the government acted, for if the church did not put an end to the plight of the under-privileged, the under-privileged would put an end to the church and quite possibly, to America.

Some other clergymen and I concluded that one of the reasons for neighborhood vandalism was that there was no place to play. We began to hound City Hall until we got playgrounds, and when we did, the rate of teenage vandalism dropped markedly. I began to feel that poverty and its attendant evils could be similarly overcome. But how could we get an indifferent society to participate?

It was then that the biblical idea of the kingdom of God suggested itself to me. The kingdom of God had been proclaimed by the Old Testament prophets as the hope of the world — a situation where personal righteousness and social justice prevailed. Unfortunately, large segments of Christianity felt that things were so bad in the world that the only way the kingdom would come would be through the special intervention of God at the end of the age. Consequently, many were not willing to do anything, feeling it was a hopeless task until God saw fit to act. For my part, I was convinced that Jesus had come to announce that the kingdom was already being inaugurated — that it was here, if we would just let it have sway in our lives. I had to acknowledge that the kingdom of God was not much in evidence at the moment, but that it could be if individual men and women would freely do God's will because they love God's will. There were, of course, social workers who were attempting to bring about a better society without religion, but I didn't hold out much hope for that. I believed that it was necessary to weld religious conviction with social concern in order to change society.

The work was hard, the hours were long, and I was grieved by the misfortunes of the people. In the winter of 1888, I was stricken with influenza. Because of the pressures of my parish, I got up too soon, and in my weakened condition, I contracted another illness that left me almost completely deaf. I felt cut off from people. I was lonely and desolate. I was shut out from the world of sound, no longer able to hear the laughter of children, the music of the human voice, the song of the birds, the rain on the roof, the crackling of a burning log, or the babbling of a brook. I withdrew temporarily from friends and associates because of our common frustration and embarrassment. I took a leave of absence from my church that I used for travel and for deeper thought. I also studied lip-reading, so that when I returned to my work, I could once again participate in social settings. Certainly, this affliction gave me greater sensitivity to all who are cut off from social contact.

In 1889, I had met a young woman, Pauline Rother, while I was visiting in Milwaukee. I was attracted to her, but because of my deafness and other complications, I did not follow up on our meeting. After several years of contact, however, I did ask her to marry me. She said "yes," and we were married in 1893. She has been my constant companion and my ears ever since. She has enabled me to accomplish whatever I have accomplished.

It was during those years in New York that several Baptist ministers joined with me in an enterprise that we called The Brotherhood of the Kingdom. It was our intention to permeate modern social movements with Jesus' teachings about the kingdom of God. We endorsed the necessity of personal salvation, but we felt that the church had focused so much attention on this that it detracted from a wider responsibility for others. We felt that Christians should care so much about others that they would not let others suffer any deprivations that would threaten them. We were concerned with securing better government and with getting better people into government. We met periodically for prayer, meditation, and discussion, and then went back to our places of employment, more determined to practice the principles of brotherhood.

In time, other ministers joined us, and then a number of lay people. We never had more than 200 members in a half-dozen cities across the country, but a number of them were in key positions and influenced their communities. Many of us wrote articles for magazines and newspapers, often championing the rights of the oppressed and the exploited. Consequently, we were seen by conservative church people as radicals and heretics who had abandoned the traditional ideas about Christianity and adopted socialistic ideas about economics. Indeed, we were socialistic, by which we meant that government had an obligation to protect the weak and the small. But the socialism we envisioned, unlike atheistic Marxism, was a system that operated from a religious base, a recognition that all of us are part of the universal family of God, a recognition that we are responsible for one another.

In 1897, the German Department of Rochester Seminary asked me to come there to teach. After eleven years serving the church in New York City, I felt I had something to share with students who would one day pastor churches, so I accepted. Five years later, I was invited to join the larger and more important English department as professor of church history. This allowed me the opportunity I needed to think, to sort through my experiences, and to put them down on paper.

In 1907, after a number of attempts, I finally finished a book titled *Christianity and the Social Crisis* and sent it off to a publisher to see if they would accept it. They did, and the book was published. In the meantime, I took my family to Germany for a one-year sabbatical. When I returned, I discovered that the book had been a phenomenal success and I had become a celebrity. For years I could scarcely keep up with the invitations to speak.

In that book, and several others that followed it, I tried to describe the kind of society I believed we could have in America if we desired it. I foresaw a day when government would provide low-cost housing so that the poor could live in healthy surroundings. I saw pensions being provided for the aged, insurance for the unemployed, medical care for all, a graduated income tax, city operation of local transportation systems, gas and electricity facilities, a work-week of fifty hours or less, laws to assure safe, clean, and humane working conditions for women, recreational facilities provided by local governments, and regulation of natural resources by the federal government. I suggested that giant corporations should come under government regulation in order to provide a fairer distribution of national wealth, that government would run parcel post for cheaper transportation of goods, and that the government would issue money orders to provide for cheaper transference of funds. I proposed that there be a League to Enforce Peace established wherein all the nations of the world could come together to settle their disputes by negotiation and arbitration. I proposed that there be an international peace keeping force to be used as a last resort to prevent nations from going to war.

Some people said I was a prophet. I simply said that these ideas were a blueprint that our country might follow to develop a society in which the poor might get a fairer shake. I was convinced that people of good will could have the kind of country I envisioned, for they had the means to get it — the vote. However, those who were well-off resisted what I had to say. They felt I was a socialist menace. But what I called for was a Christian socialism. I felt that religion must be the motivation for all personal and public conduct or else socialism would decay into Marxism — a godless dictatorship of savagely selfish people determined to rule the world on their own brutal terms.

I also knew that such changes would come about slowly and gradually. Therefore, I was prepared to plant the seeds and to wait for others to espouse my ideas, and many did. In 1908, the Methodist Episcopal Church made its first social declaration built on my proposals. In 1909, that church adopted its social creed, again based on my thoughts. Subsequently, the Presbyterian, Congregational, and Northern Baptist Churches adopted the ideas of that Methodist Creed. The Federal Council of Churches, organized in 1908, representing 31 Protestant denominations, adopted much of the Methodist Social Creed as a statement of the social conscience of the Protestant Churches in America. Whatever happens to me, I feel that the fire I ignited will live on in the social witness of the Christian Churches of America.

It was a time of unbounded optimism. I felt we were all called to be workers for God's kingdom. Some of us felt that kingdom could become a full-fledged reality in our time. If it were to happen anywhere, it would be in America.

In 1914, the optimism that many of us felt was given a severe blow. A shot was fired in Sarajevo which drew all of Europe into a great war. Our dreams about the coming kingdom began to crumble. My study of history had convinced me that, whatever the battle cry, wars are fought for economic reasons. This one also was a battle for power and money. I spoke and wrote openly against both sides, warning that war on such a basis would only be the first of many. America was not yet in the war, but America was profiting from the munitions traffic and it was clear that America favored Britain. I publicly stated that whatever profit we made out of the sale of munitions would be paid for by us over and over. But Americans, so recently victorious in the Spanish-American War, now saw themselves as a world power and were anxious to get into the war.

I loved America, but I appreciated Germany's culture. I could not join in a fanatical partisanship against Germany. I had a German name, I spoke German, I had lived in Germany, so I was accused of being a German sympathizer. People who had once shared my vision of peace and America's place as a peacemaker, now turned against me. Speaking engagements were cancelled. I was not pro-German, I was pro-Christian. I called for Christians to be the gyroscope of a world that was passing through a storm. At all costs, I felt that America must stay out of the war. My own son hurried off to France to join a volunteer ambulance corps. He couldn't wait to become involved. As far as I was concerned, America's involvement in the war would be a negation of Christianity and of the social progress that many of us felt had been taking place.

When America did enter the war in 1917, I was convinced that we had forfeited our destiny to be peacemakers and heralds of God's kingdom. When I received the news that we had joined the conflict I said, "I will mourn for my country as long as I live." From that day to this, I have worn a black suit every day with a piece of crepe on the lapel.

I must confess, in closing, that I have been impatient. I know that social change comes gradually, but we were so tantalizingly close to great social accomplishments that I ached to see them instituted quickly. What will be the outcome of this tragic war, I do not know. I am sure there will be no real winners. I know that the advancement of God's kingdom has been set back by it. Still, each of you has a part to play in advancing that kingdom. When you make it your business to see that the hungry are fed, the homeless are provided for, the ill-clothed are provided with clothing, the abused are given refuge, the disadvantaged are treated fairly, and the outsider receives justice, you are building the kind of world Jesus envisioned when he taught us to pray, "Thy kingdom come, thy will be done on earth as it already is in heaven."

A Righteous Gentile:
Raoul Wallenberg

John 15:12-17

Do you see this briefcase? It contains money. Lots of money. I intend to use it to get whatever I can for the Jewish refugees left in Budapest. Tomorrow I will meet with Marshall Malinovsky, the leader of the Soviet army, whose troops are now in control of the city. The remaining German soldiers have given up, but the Hungarian fascists, who call themselves the Arrow Cross, still have snipers in the city, so I have to travel to the city of Debrecen, some 120 miles away, to meet with the marshall. He has sent an armed escort to accompany me, and to tell you the truth, I don't know whether I am to be protected or arrested.

My name is Raoul Wallenberg. I arrived here in Hungary in July 1944, and today is January 16, 1945, so that means I have been doing this refugee work less than seven months — but it feels like a lifetime. Let me tell you what has happened.

I guess I need to begin with my early life, because whatever has taken place has been the result of connections that developed early. I was born in Sweden in 1912 into a well-to-do and influential family. The Wallenbergs are well known as diplomats and bankers. Some call us the Swedish Rockefellers. My father, a naval officer, died when I was an infant, so I was raised by my mother and grandparents. My grandfather took charge of my education. As a result, I spent time in Germany and France, and became fluent in German, French, English, and Russian. I was raised in the Lutheran church, and that training has influenced the way I see the world and our responsibilities for one another. I studied architecture at the University of Michigan, but when

Sweden did not recognize my credentials, I gave in to my grandfather's wishes and entered into the family's banking enterprise, taking an assignment in South Africa.

Subsequently, I was sent to Palestine and worked at a bank in Haifa. While there I met several Jews who had fled Nazi oppression in Germany. Hitler hated the Jews. He felt that they were responsible for Germany's defeat in World War I, for communism, and for high unemployment in Germany. Nazi gangs roamed streets in German cities, beating Jews, and as Germans began to occupy other countries of Europe, anti-Semitism spread.

In 1938, my grandfather died, and I felt free to move into a different business. I became director of an import company owned by a Jewish man living in Sweden. This allowed me to travel throughout Europe, and I saw firsthand what was happening to Jews. As a child I had memorized passages from the Bible that reminded us of justice and righteousness and suggested that all of us are children of God. I could not accept what was happening to the Jews. That same year a conference of leading nations met to decide what to do about Jews who were trying to escape Nazi terror. Most countries decided that they could not take in many Jews. As German occupation of other countries continued, Jewish populations were gathered up and imprisoned. Some stories began to leak out that Jews were actually being killed. Free countries were not sure they could believe it.

About that time a movie titled *Pimpernel Smith* was made. It was an update of a previous story, *The Scarlet Pimpernel*. In this movie the hero almost effortlessly rescued people from the Nazis. I remember telling my sister that was exactly the kind of thing I would like to do. Little did I dream that such an opportunity would open for me.

Unknown to the rest of the world, on January 20, 1942, at a house outside of Berlin, Nazi leaders gathered to decide on what they called "a final solution" to the Jewish question.

The decision was to round up every Jew in Europe and to send them to extermination camps. By 1944 the Nazis were well on their way to accomplishing their goal. They turned their attention on Hungary, an ally of Germany that had the largest intact Jewish community in Europe — perhaps 750,000 people. In March of that year, Adolph Eichmann, a colonel in the German SS, arrived in Budapest and prepared to deport and annihilate all the Jews in Hungary. By June 13, 147 trains had carried 437,000 Hungarian Jews to Auschwitz and other extermination camps. His plan called for a final and complete roundup by July 6, 1944.

Meanwhile, in the United States, President Roosevelt set up a War Refugee Board to assist the growing number of European war refugees and to aid the remnant of European Jewry. The free world was dismayed by the things they were hearing, and President Roosevelt declared that, following the war, anyone found guilty of war crimes would be tried as a criminal. The War Refugee Board needed someone to go to Hungary to see what could be done. United States officials approached Sweden, which was the most important neutral country having reasonably good relations with Germany. My employer, who was a Hungarian Jew, recommended me.

When I was approached, I accepted eagerly. I knew that time was running out for the Jews. I insisted that I must have diplomatic status, freedom to act independently from the Swedish embassy in Budapest, and lots of money to bribe officials and to buy what would be necessary. President Roosevelt agreed, and so did the Swedish Foreign Office. I was to spend July learning about the situation, but as I read about Jews being crammed into cattle cars with doors nailed shut, and no food, water, or sanitary facilities for five days, only to arrive at camps where 6,000 were gassed and burned each day, I had to act more quickly. I prayed, "Dear God, help those people. Help me to help them."

I arrived in Budapest as a Swedish diplomat on July 9. Eichmann's timetable had been slowed because international pressure was causing the leader of the Hungarian puppet government, Admiral Horthy, to slow down the deportations. But Horthy was on a slippery slope. Hungarian fascists, the Arrow Cross, who were fully as ruthless as the Nazis, were quite willing to seize power and turn all authority over to their Nazi allies. Jews needed to have some kind of safety net.

I decided to take advantage of the German penchant for bureaucracy and following orders. I designed a protective passport, called a *schutzpass*, to show that the bearer was in transit to Sweden and was under Swedish protection. Many German soldiers and their Hungarian backups would be poorly educated young men who would be impressed by an official-looking document. We had posters of passes printed to make sure that soldiers would be familiar with them. I then pressured the Hungarian Foreign Ministry to allow us to distribute 1,500 of the passes. We eventually increased the number to 4,500. When I say I pressured officials, I mean I did whatever I had to do: cajole, argue, threaten, bribe. The money made available to me was often used for the latter. With that money I also set up soup kitchens all over Budapest to feed Jewish people who were cut off from their resources. During the next few months I purchased some thirty buildings to be used as soup kitchens, safe houses, hospitals, and orphanages for people under Swedish protection. Sometimes, I went to the railroad station and handed the passes to those being prepared to board trains. Within weeks, thousands had been saved through use of the passes, but we couldn't save everyone. We had permission to distribute 4,500 such passes. We distributed three times that number. It became increasingly difficult to get the passes printed, so eventually we printed up hundreds of simplified documents, and even they worked wonders. Other neutral embassies in Budapest saw what we were doing, and they, too, began to distribute protective passes. Eventually, we had 35,000 persons in our protective houses and 5,000 children in our orphanages.

On one occasion, I boarded a train that was already loaded with people to be deported, and I began to hand out the passes. An SS officer ordered me to stop. He even shot over my head. I continued to distribute the passes and then ordered all pass holders to leave the train and go to a caravan of cars bearing Swedish colors. The Nazis seemed too stunned to do anything.

I interviewed five men who had escaped from a Nazi death camp. They told me what was going on in those camps. I had their stories sent to governments and newspapers around the world. The United States, Sweden, Britain, the pope, and the International Red Cross pressured Admiral Horthy to suspend the deportations. A new deportation had been set by Eichmann for August 25. Romania surrendered to the Allies on August 24 and declared war on Hungary. Admiral Horthy was aware that the Germans were losing the war. Even in Germany, Heinrich Himmler, head of the Gestapo, sensing that Germany might lose the war, cabled Eichmann to desist. Eichmann and his death squads withdrew and returned to Germany. I cultivated whatever contacts I had with Hungarian officials and promised them that if they would help me to save Jews, I would see that they were saved from the Soviets when the war was over. It looked as though our work would soon be over.

Some officials were helpful, but the Arrow Cross, the Hungarian fascists, were not about to moderate. On October 15, Admiral Horthy announced his intention to surrender to the Soviets. Upon hearing that, the Arrow Cross seized power. Bands of thugs roamed the streets, looting Jewish residences and killing Jews wherever they found them. I continued to distribute passes that by now had become photostats with my signature.

We gave passes to all who requested them. On one occasion the fascists were holding 5,000 Jews in a synagogue. I marched in with a Swiss diplomat and urged all who had Swiss papers to hold them up, form a column, and follow me. Hundreds held up any paper they had and followed us to safety.

With the fascists in control, Eichmann was invited back. Germany, needing its trains for the war effort, could no longer make trains available to transport Jews out of Hungary. Eichmann's new plan, therefore, was to round up Jews and march them to the border, where they would be picked up by German trains. He announced that the new government would no longer recognize protective passes issued by foreign governments. I had occasion to speak with the wife of the Arrow Cross Minister of Foreign Affairs, telling her that at war's end her husband would be shot as a war criminal if the passes were not honored. He subsequently announced that the passes would be honored.

Eichmann began the death marches on November 8. Women and children were forced to make the 125 mile march in freezing sleet and snow. Any who fell were shot or beaten to death. Some froze to death; some committed suicide. The suffering was unimaginable. Often my helpers and I would drive out to give food, help, and encouragement as people made the long march. We insisted that pass holders be turned over to us. Sometimes I would walk among the deportees and say, "Don't I know you? Didn't I give you a pass?" They would offer any sheet of paper, which I would pocket, and then I would tell them to get in line to be transported back to Budapest. Amazingly, time and again, the German and Hungarian soldiers, who were used to obeying orders, released prisoners to our custody.

Under intense international pressure, the Arrow Cross government was obliged to call a halt to the death marches. Eichmann once again managed to get some trains provided for his evil purpose. Even with the Soviets closing in on the city, he was determined to deport 63,000 Jews he had sealed up in the Jewish ghetto in Budapest. We still had 30,000 people sheltered in our Swedish safe houses, but their future was uncertain. Eichmann was determined to kill every Jew in the city. He wanted me dead, too, but the Nazis were unwilling to do anything that might damage their relationship with Sweden, as Sweden represented German interests in many countries.

In early December, I invited Eichmann to dinner. I hoped to frighten him into ending his reign of terror by pointing out how close the Soviets were to Budapest. He told me that he knew that he would be killed when the Soviets took the city, but he enjoyed his power. He warned me that even a neutral diplomat could meet with an accident if he were not careful. A few days later a truck drove into my car and destroyed it. Fortunately, I was not in it. I knew that the Nazis intended to get me, so from then on I slept in a different place each night. A police official, who finally became revolted by the slaughter, provided me with a bodyguard and kept me informed of the intentions of the death squads so that we could move people to safety.

Eichmann finally left Budapest on December 23, but he left orders with his Nazi soldiers to kill every Jew in the central ghetto. A new wave of terror was unleashed. Even while Budapest was under siege, nearly 15,000 Jews were murdered. When I was informed that the SS general who was in charge of destroying Jews was about to launch his attack on the ghetto, I sent him a message: "If you do not stop this now, I guarantee that you will be hanged as a war criminal." He called off the massacre, those Jews were spared, and two days later the Soviets entered the city and ended the Nazi terror. Nearly 100,000 Hungarian Jews had been saved. And that just about brings us to this present moment. Even before the Soviets entered the city, I had been contacting international organizations for help in reuniting refugees with their families and to see to the food and medicine needs of those in our safe houses after the liberation. I knew that we would need the cooperation of the Soviets, so I contacted a Soviet army officer, told him our story, and asked permission to go to speak with Marshall Malinovsky in Debrecen. I hope that with the funds in this briefcase, I can secure the things our refugees need for their continued survival.

Some of my associates have told me not to go. The Soviets are such an unknown quantity. But what choice do I have? The needs of the survivors are enormous. They need a spokesman, for we do not know how the Hungarian authorities will respond to them. I have never felt that neutrality was a comfortable, easy way to avoid suffering. I have been here to participate in the suffering of the Hungarian people. We have no guarantees that helping others will exempt us from suffering, but if we are decent human beings who acknowledge that we are all part of one family, we must offer one another whatever help we can. I call that love, and I am reminded of the words of Jesus who said, "No one has greater love than this, to lay down one's life for one's friends." May all of us be able to live up to such a standard if it becomes necessary.

Epilogue
Raoul Wallenberg bid farewell to his associates with the intention of returning in a few days. He was taken into custody by the Soviets, who soon denied knowing anything about him. Subsequently, they acknowledged that he had died in 1947 in a Soviet prison. Others have reported that he was still alive in the

1950s, 1960s, and 1970s. It is not known why he was arrested. Russian authorities have given no further information. The people of Israel call him "a righteous Gentile."

Angelo Roncalli from Sotto il Monte: Pope John XXIII

Ephesians 2:13-22

What would you look for in a reformation? Immediate changes? Apparent victory for one side and apparent defeat for another? Revolutionary change of authority? Transference of power? I have been part of a reformation, but it had none of these characteristics. When you think of reformation you probably call to mind the Protestant Reformation of 1517. I would like to tell you about a far more recent reformation in the Roman Catholic church which is bringing about great change.

What do you think are the characteristics of a reformer? Aggressive? Ambitious? Self-assertive? Zealous? Young? Fire-eyed? Revolutionary? One who topples authority? Some people have called me a reformer, but none of those characteristics apply to me.

I want to tell you about a reformation with which you may not be well-acquainted — a reformation that is still going on. I want to tell you this so that you can have some appreciation for the way God is at work today in the church. In order to do this, I need to tell you something about the life of this one they call the reformer — about myself. I apologize for mentioning myself, for I am the least of all God's servants, but I am emboldened to speak because I want you to understand that God can use the least and the lowliest to accomplish God's great purposes, if we will allow God to operate in our lives. I trust that you will indulge an old man's desire to speak and that you will accept whatever I say as coming from one whose only desire is to glorify God.

In order that you may understand how marvelously God works, I would like to tell you first about my simple beginnings. I was born in the tiny village of Sotto il Monte in northern Italy, in 1881. The name means, "Under the Mountain." To call it a village is to overstate the case — there were about two dozen houses in all. I was named Angelo Roncalli, a name I imagine you have never heard before. My family was poor and large, and there was little prospect for improvement. Our house overlooked the small village church of St. Giovanni Battista — St. John the Baptist — a name that embedded itself in my mind. As a child, I used to watch the priest coming and going on his pastoral rounds, and by the age of six I decided I wanted to be a priest. I was fond of the old parish priest, and desired to be like him. With his help, I was able to enter what we called a college at the age of ten to prepare for the priesthood. A year later, I went to the junior seminary in the large city of Bergamo.

In 1895, I entered the major seminary at Bergamo to prepare more earnestly for my priestly career. While I was a good student, I was also judgmental of the lives of others, a chatterbox, and a gossip. I often had to pray for the grace to keep my mouth shut. The three best students at our seminary were chosen each year to go for further study in Rome. I had no reason to expect that I would make it, especially since I had offended people by some of the things I had said, but at the age of nineteen I was one who was chosen. This was already more than I had ever dreamed could happen — a country peasant sent to be educated at the headquarters of the church. The seminary was completely out of the mainstream of life; it was an academic institution run by scholars who gave the students little preparation for life in the parish.

In 1903, at the age of 22, I was ordained sub-deacon. This carried with it the decision for celibacy. That same year I was awarded my doctorate in theology. In 1904, I was ordained a priest. Who would have imagined that I would come this far? I felt that I was at the height of my career! I was now in a position to use my education to get ahead, and

I had a constant battle within myself to hold my youthful ambition in check.

My first sermon was to an audience of girls and ladies. I had well-prepared notes, but I lost my place and everything I wanted to say got turned around; it was a complete disaster. I wanted to quit the priesthood, feeling it was not for me, but my senior pastor encouraged me to stay. Shortly thereafter, I became secretary to the Bishop of Bergamo, and with that my activities as a parish priest came to an end.

Next I must tell you about some of the things that were taking place in the church. Many scholars, priests, and laymen were calling for a greater openness in the church, especially with regard to biblical scholarship. Protestant scholars were making tremendous contributions in biblical criticism, and a number of Roman Catholics were championing that cause. The bureaucracy of the church, however, viewed all this with suspicion. This new point of view was called modernism, and the central authority of our church, the Curia, would have none of it. The church was more intent on idealizing the past, rejecting the present, and fearing the future. Pope Pius X was prevailed upon to condemn modernism and to excommunicate some of its proponents. As a consequence, some of the finest minds in the church were forced to leave the church or to remain and be silent. There was a period of heresy hunting, and those priests who did not conform were subject to transfer or career interruption. I did not speak on the issue, but there were those in the Curia who suspected me of modernistic thought. I saw in this situation how important it would be to open the church to the modern world. I saw the dangers of a narrow rigidity, but I was powerless to do anything about it.

The years before the First World War were years of great social unrest. The bishop under whom I worked at Bergamo was a great social liberal. He encouraged me to become involved in social issues. Even though I was his secretary, I taught history at the seminary and sided with strikers who were seeking the right to organize. I traveled with the bishop to France and Palestine, all of which opened my eyes to the situations of people elsewhere.

When my bishop died in 1915, it was apparent that my prospects for advancement were over. I was thought to be a liberal, but no longer under a liberal bishop's protection. When World War I broke out, I was drafted, serving in Bergamo, first in a medical unit, then as a chaplain in a military hospital. I continued to teach in the seminary at night.

After the war, I was made spiritual director of the seminary, but my ideas were suspect, so I was not appointed to teach. I spent my time helping to organize women's groups and labor unions. I was involved in raising money for a student hostel. At that time I made a vow never to push myself in ecclesiastical circles, never to ask for an assignment, never to seek recognition or position. My motto became "obedience and peace." Surprisingly, I was invited to Rome to become a fund-raiser for our missionary program. With that post I received the title "monsignor." I am sure that those who suspected my liberal ideas thought that fund-raising would keep me from corrupting others.

I must now tell you about some experiences I had outside of Italy, for though I thought that I was often working in backwater towns, I now believe that even in those places God was training me for what was yet to be. I worked in Rome as a mission fund-raiser from 1921 to 1925. I was briefly appointed as a professor at one of the seminaries, but there were fears that I was a modernist, so quite suddenly, I was appointed as papal visitor to Bulgaria. Since I was a representative of the pope, I was consecrated as a bishop and given the rank of Archbishop. But was it a promotion? Less than 1% of Bulgaria was Roman Catholic! I had no particular talents for the position; I was just picked to fill a spot. I was to report on the situation of Roman Catholics in that country and on any possibilities of union with the Orthodox church, which represented 85% of the people. My stay in Eastern Europe could have been a short one. In fact, it lasted twenty years. I learned much from my stay there. I studied the Bulgarian language, which pleased the people, Catholic and otherwise. I visited among the people and learned about their lives. I also learned what it is like to be a minority. I discovered how meaningful it could be for people if they could participate in the services of worship in their own language. I developed a respect and an affection for people of other traditions: Orthodox, Greeks, and Turks. I learned to emphasize the things that we held in common, rather than to focus on what divided us. From my own church I learned patience: my duties were ill-defined; I had little status; I wanted to be doing more, but Rome took little notice of me. On occasion, it would be rumored that I was to be appointed to a more prestigious position in Bucharest or Istanbul, but nothing came of it. I distrusted my own ambition and remained firm in my conviction that I would never ask for a change. God can teach us many things if we are open and adaptable.

In 1934, I was appointed papal delegate to Istanbul. There was only a small population of Catholics there, but I was satisfied. I learned the Turkish language and instituted its use in the liturgy of the church. That impressed the Turks, but it displeased many Catholics, who had grown up hearing Latin. This was an issue yet to be faced by the whole church.

During the Second World War, events were to create a change for me. The Vatican has diplomatic relations with numerous countries — among them, at the time, was France. France was governed by the puppet government set up by the German's at Vichy. Our Papal diplomat, called a Nuncio, had, of course, dealt with the Vichy government. But in 1944, DeGaulle and the Free French were about to resume control in France, and the previous Nuncio would not be tolerated.

The church needed an untainted and unknown representative in France, and I was chosen. Pope Pius XII himself made the appointment. It was a considerable personal promotion. It was not easy to be a diplomat. Though talkative by nature, I had to learn to be reserved. I was concerned to do and to say what was politically safe, but I was also a representative of Christ, and therefore, I tried to be truthful. I learned to give up my own tastes and wishes in order to serve what I felt was the will of God. I was by nature outgoing, and therefore made friends with numerous people. Even with unbelievers there was warm and mutual respect. I think I can say that I was liked and trusted, but I must also say that I was probably not taken very seriously. People thought of me as a jolly, likeable, affectionate, roly-poly Italian. I spent eight years in France, doing my best not to present my own views, but to represent Pius XII. My critics in the Roman Curia discounted my work because they felt my style was too simple.

In 1953, at the age of 71, my life changed again. I was appointed Patriarch of Venice, and with it I was given the title of cardinal — prince of the church. What an enormous honor to be bestowed on a simple peasant boy from Sotto il Monte! I had come to the top of the ecclesiastical ladder in the very province where I had been born, and none of the steps had been chosen by me, except the first: to be a priest. My one desire now was to be a holy pastor for whatever years remained to me. I felt inadequate to meet the great demands of being a patriarch. My intention was to live by love and humility. There were those who equated my simplicity of style with stupidity and ignorance. Nevertheless, I was determined to pursue mildness, patience, and charity, for I was convinced that that is the course Jesus would have us follow.

I had developed great respect for Christians of other persuasions, and I was often involved in meetings on Christian unity. At one such meeting, I pointed out that "the road to unity between the different Christian creeds is love, so little practiced on either side."

In 1958, Pius XII died at the age of 82. At 77, I was only five years younger. I left at once for Rome to attend the funeral and to participate in the College of Cardinals, which would elect another pope. Technically, any Catholic may be pope, but traditionally, a cardinal is elected. Archbishop Montini of Milan had been groomed by Pius XII, but unfortunately, he had not yet been made a cardinal, and was, therefore, technically not available. The cardinals felt that what was needed was a caretaker pope, someone who would not live too long and thereby get in the way of Montini's election next time.

Well, the one qualification I had was great age: I wouldn't be around too long and I was virtually unknown. That seems to have cinched my election. Not a very complimentary reason for being chosen, I will grant you. I acknowledged my own unworthiness, and yet, humbly accepted the election. I took the name John XXIII for several reasons: for one thing, it had been my father's name, and it was the name of the church in the village where I had grown up. It was also the name that had been used most by previous popes, and I was quick to point out that all of them had had short reigns.

In the sermon I delivered upon my election, I spoke much of love. That speech was to be the manifesto of my reign. I determined to capitalize on my most abundant characteristic: ordinariness. I wanted people to know that the pope was servant of the servants of God. It was a heady business being at the helm of the church. In fact, I would often have to say to myself, "Don't take yourself so seriously, Angelo." Sometimes I would be preoccupied about something and I would think, "I'll speak to the Pope about it." Then I would remember that *I* am the pope. My usual solution was, "Well then, I'll speak to God about it." I wanted to be where the people were, so I made frequent trips in and out of the city of Rome. I discarded the traditional silk slippers for sturdy shoes so that I could get out and walk among the people.

I saw many needs for reform in the church, but I was also aware that it must come through the machinery of the institution. Therefore, soon after my election, I presented to the cardinals in the Curia my idea that a council should be called for the purpose of revising canon, or church, law. The idea met with complete silence. The cardinals felt that there was no need for a council; the pope had complete authority to deal with doctrine. But I persisted. I felt that the idea was not mine, that it was the result of inspiration, and that I was simply an instrument of God put in this place, at this time, for this reason.

Reluctantly, acknowledging that a Council of Bishops would take place, the members of the Curia began to prepare position papers, which they expected the council simply to endorse. The members of the Curia were good men; they loved the church; but they loved it as it had been, and they could not see what it was called for. I set the theme with the word *aggiornamento* meaning "modernization" — but to the Curia that meant merely streamlining the old methods and old statements of doctrine. The conservative members of the Curia feared that a council would undermine the discipline and unity of the church by diluting papal authority. I had to explain to them that it is love that matters, that love is the foundation of the church. The pope is the vicar of Christ's *love*, not of his *power*.

The council was announced on Christmas Day 1961. It was set to convene in October 1962. The request for ideas as to what should be dealt with brought an input from around the world that filled 2,000 files. When the council met, we were aware that what we were dealing with was significant for the whole Christian church, so we invited observers from other Christian denominations around the world and saw to it that they had the best seats. The gathering came to be called

Vatican II since it was the second Council to meet in Vatican City, the first having met in 1869. The items to be dealt with eventually revolved around the liturgy of the church, the nature of the church, ecumenism (that is, relations among the denominations), and the sources of revelation. After considerable discussion and debate, statements on each of these topics were to be redrafted and presented at a second session in 1963.

The results of all this will have to be assessed in the decades to come. I consider what took place there to be a reformation of the church that has altered things in such a way that they will never be the same again. Things were set in motion in 1962 that have yet to be fully realized. Perhaps what emanated from Vatican II is as much in the form of attitude as it is a statement in print. The liturgy is now in the language of the people instead of in Latin. There is greater participation by the laity, as is the case among Protestants. The idea of the church has been broadened so that we have come to see all Christians as brothers and sisters in Christ. There is a greater emphasis on scripture as opposed to tradition. There is an openness to collegiality, that is, consensus among the leaders of the church, instead of the absolute rule of one man or of the Curia. There has been a movement toward love, concern, and involvement in the needs and problems of the whole human race.

Yes, it was a reformation, not a revolution. It initiated a definite positive change of attitude from within the church. I think that it has been good for the church, and I am grateful that I, Angelo Roncalli, John XXIII, from Sotto il Monte, was given opportunity to be in on it.

CPSIA information can be obtained
at www.ICGtesting.com
Printed in the USA
FFOW01n0558100617
36484FF